ANXIETY REWIRE YOUR BRAIN

Understand How To Stop The Mind Out Of Control In Moments Of Severe Anxiety Or Severe Panic Attacks. Transform Personality Disorder And Resume Rationality. Solution Therapy

HENRY BISHOP

Disclaimer

All knowledge contained in this book is given for informational and educational purposes only. The author is not in any way accountable for any results or outcomes that emanate from using this material. Constructive attempts have been made to provide information that is both accurate and effective, but the author is not bound for the accuracy or use/misuse of this information.

INTRODUCTION

Anxiety attacks are one of the most severe conditions you have to deal with, and unexpected and unresolved cases of extreme terror are triggered for no apparent reason.

Several cases of anxiety have been studied and treated to show that anxiety therapy is not just about reducing general anxiety levels. In a real anxiety attack, this help is more about dealing with the topic.

After you decide on an anxiety attack, you need to know the cause of the panic that got you to the point of an anxiety attack. You need to understand that treating anxiety is only possible if you find the cause of this terrible condition. Those words are consistent with the fact that you must find the root cause of your depression to get rid of the addictions that are causing disasters in your own life.

Once you know the cause of depression, the answer is not to examine it and think about it. It's better to stick to self-help strategies and free yourself from the vicious cycle of anxiety and anxiety attacks. It is also known as the "vicious circle" because anxiety and panic cause you to spin until you are destroyed. The impact of disasters on a patient's health and life is one of the most dangerous consequences of an anxiety attack.

Many self-help anxieties can play an active role in treating anxiety, from cognitive and behavioural therapy to relaxation techniques, breathing techniques, and, ultimately, treatment if all other methods do not reduce anxiety attacks.

Evidence in this field shows that drugs are often used to treat anxiety because doctors who treat illness see this as the easiest way to control the disease. At this point, however, you need to know that medicine is never a way to cure your anxiety. It only preys on you but does not separate you from it. The treatment also has the potential to cause side effects.

Many popular approaches to self-help depression include meditation, yoga, aerobics, etc., daily and weekly exercise, and healthy eating - a balanced diet.

These are probably some of the most common approaches that you might try to overcome with anxiety. However, they still seem to be looking for unique self-help methods for anxiety that can reach new levels beyond anxiety.

The pain and trauma of an anxiety attack are seen in people with anxiety, mental illness, health, and even the personality of a panic person. Many of you may be quiet and jeopardize different opportunities.

Modern and innovative methods for reducing anxiety still brighten their faces in the hope that they, too, can lead a healthy, high-quality life through panic.

Remember that anxiety attacks are significant for a healthy lifestyle. Let's get started.

CHAPTER ONE

MANAGING AND UNDERSTANDING ANXIETY

The experience of anxiety is general and universal. It is an inevitable part of the human situation. It is characterized by confusion and tension at all levels of life - from foreign and state to domestic and personal. Many may reject their anxiety or at least their frequency (even for themselves) for various reasons, such as the desire to avoid humiliation, arrogance, fear of rejection, risk, and fear of vulnerability, etc.

Anxiety is disturbing and deteriorating. Crippling perseverance. During everyday life marked by sadness, conflict, and misfortune, it is inevitable to stress. We can relate anxiety to psychological stress, which manifests itself in anxiety, irritability, anticipation, or discomfort. Mental stress arises either from feelings of confusion about the future or future events or from feelings of being unable to regulate one's environment or status.

Anxiety is a natural emotional response for people who want to live comfortably. Anxiety is a reminder of a terrible human fragility and total impotence to control his destiny. It is a survival mechanism because it increases self-defence. However, Anxiety reflects a warning sign to increase fainting to survive. It is said that anxiety spreads thinly; Not every anxiety is dangerous, just a specific type.

Secular and religious psychologists generally believe that sometimes mild anxiety leads to productivity. Anxiety increases, enthusiasm increases, and concentration increases.

Therefore, one's skills and abilities are used more effectively. Indeed, severe educational and social impacts can occur when there is no anxiety (e.g., criminal hardcore behavior) or when anxiety is excessive (such as typical sensitive children in a destructive home).

The relationship between friendly and dangerous anxiety is similar to stress and need. Medium pressure is required for performance and high performance. This is especially true when athletes are ready to take part in or take part in field events.

However, health hazards arise when stress turns into stress. This can happen to a manager who needs regular compliance goals and irreconcilable deadlines to meet them. Alternative anxiety classifications can help. There are two types of debilitating anxiety: fundamental and neurotic. Simple anxiety is the acute psychological distress that many people experience in their lives. Neurotic anxiety is the emotional distress that has become an essential characteristic of one's actions.

Neurosis is a constant psychological disorder that covers all people.

Many neuroses include compulsive behaviour, paranoia, phobias, aggression, neurasthenia, chronic depression, and more. Untreated neurosis can go wild, although it usually depends on heredity and predisposition. The treatment of neurotic anxiety involves a specialized approach because anxiety is comfortably consolidated. There is also a need to overcome personality defects.

It is essential to identify and study the causal and psychodynamic factors that underlie anxiety, which may require detailed discussion and analysis of children's experiences and learn at home.

Psychosomatic symptoms such as frequent stomach pain, palpitations, headaches, muscles, and various physical pain can be associated with specific manifestations of anxiety. Persistent or persistent depression causes a decrease in physical health. The long-term effects are organic and functional diseases ranging from dyspepsia to heart disease.

Anxiety can also cause severe psycho-emotional disorders. Initially, anxiety reduces effectiveness by increasing thinking skills, weakening creative thinking, and generally avoid it. Then disorientation and depression can occur.

It can also result in slowed interpersonal growth. Highly anxious people can avoid social contact, even with trusted friends, to reduce anxiety. Social contact creates feelings of confusion, mistrust, and discomfort. Natural reactions are social withdrawal and alienation.

Safety and harmony are seen as products of separation and loneliness. Therefore, the growth of interpersonal skills and social etiquette can be hampered. People who are very afraid of learning to live alone.

Psychodynamic anxiety of the underlying complex. In general, some therapists classify anxiety as an implicit and ambiguous sensation without specific sources or causes. This assertion can undoubtedly be questioned. Anxiety is usually associated with cause and effect, although the cause may be hidden or misunderstood.

CAUSES OF ANXIETY

In this chapter, I will explain the three most common forms of anxiety (including social anxiety, the anxiety of results and anxiety of choice) and the five leading causes of anxiety (including genetics, nutrition, psychology, history, and environment).

Anxiety disorders affect about 13 to 18 per cent of the total population, but we all live in various types of anxiety. Feelings of discomfort often characterize anxiety. These are often forward-looking, so our concern is about potential threats or negative experiences that have not yet occurred.

In the real world, most of us have different anxiety states, depending on the situation. That is not always a bad thing because some uncertainty will inspire us to reschedule or rethink the situation before we act. However, excessive anxiety can paralyze to the point where we cannot decide, take action, or confuse the event.

Depending on what causes anxiety, there may be various forms of anxiety. These three forms of anxiety are the most common types mentioned in psychological research today, although there may be other types of anxiety that do not fit this definition (existential anxiety, specific phobias, the anxiety of death, etc.).

However, this is a concern that I will list in this chapter. We may not be calm or avoid situations involving large groups of people (such as class, work, public speaking, school meetings, etc.), or we may feel uncomfortable or even avoid other forms of one-on-one contact (such as interviews or dating, first time communicating with a friend or meeting a celebrity).

Many people have some anxiety in this case, but they differ significantly between individuals. Many people in the group may feel more comfortable while others feel better during one-on-one interactions. Other people may feel more comfortable talking with friends, while others may feel more comfortable when they meet someone. It depends on the environment and humans.

Anxiety about performance in contrast to social anxiety, anxiety about performance is fear or anxiety of achievement, for example, when a student takes a final exam at school or a musician performs on stage.

We worry that we will not do our best or interfere or fail, and this fear can prevent us from doing our best (or even do something, for example, because there is too much stage fright).

Instead of focusing on what we have to do, we focus more on everything wrong. This can sometimes be a fulfilled prophecy. Our thoughts make us uncomfortable, unprepared, and then lead to actions that strengthen our previous perception.

Preference for anxiety is an emotion rooted in anxiety when making decisions. The reality is that none of us can act with full knowledge of the consequences or make decisions; This world is too big, and our minds cannot fully understand it. This is why we are often afraid to make crucial decisions in our lives because we do not know whether we made the best choice.

Throughout our lives, we have to make several important decisions, including what tertiary institution we are going to, what career we are pursuing, who we are going to marry, where we live, the type of car we drive, etc.

We make decisions every day and face the "potential costs" that come with choosing one choice from another. Some research shows that the more decisions we have to make, the harder it is to make decisions. We argue that the more options we have, the more "choices" cost (theoretically, the more we have to choose, the more we lose), and when prices are too high for this opportunity, we are often paralyzed. The ANXIETY of discussion makes us unable to make decisions because we have lost so much in doing the right thing.

I am sure you have experienced similar fears at various levels of your life. That's good. Many of our depression can be natural and healthy. But if it affects our way of life, it can be a dilemma we have to deal with.

The first step in solving this problem is to identify some of the possible causes of our suffering and then find the best way to overcome them. Many factors can cause our depression (and especially for our mental health). In this chapter, I will discuss some common causes of anxiety and some possible treatments.

However, it is essential to remember that because of the different factors that can trigger our fears, it is often better to combine several treatment options actively. Several gene variants can be associated with higher anxiety levels. We have different biological properties, and sometimes people experience increased anxiety for no other reason than because they are embedded in their genetic code. These genes cause chemical imbalances in your anxiety in the brain.

Treatment Options: If your biology causes your anxiety, a professional psychiatrist can prescribe medication. However, keep in mind that many of these medicines can have side effects (you can take several different drugs before you find the best - a good psychiatrist can help you with this).

Also, keep in mind that if your anxiety is triggered by a cause other than medicine, it will only function as a quick fix, but it won't solve more deep-rooted problems in your life. You may need to add other medication to your prescription.

Health anxieties can also be caused by the inactivity of the body and improper nutrition. If we don't treat our bodies properly, it can often affect our minds.

If we don't get all the nutrients, we need and eat well, that often means our brains don't eat right. It affects our minds as efficiently as possible, which can lead to higher levels of ANXIETY.

Physical activity is also significant for our physical and mental health. Playing, exercising, going to the gym, dancing, and whatever you do is the perfect way to get rid of the stresses and anxieties that can develop for days and weeks.

It is essential to be able to regulate hormones (such as adrenaline and cortisol) positively and healthily; otherwise, they will become overworked and afraid.

If you don't treat your body well anymore, you might be surprised at how much less stress and depression, you are if you take better care of your health.

Consider doing small things, e.g., substitute soda for water, eat less cake, run a few times a week, or be more aware of what you eat and feel better physically and mentally.

SYMPTOMS OF ANXIETY ATTACK

Nothing can change your life as fast as anxiety attacks can. Today's depression is a global problem. It affects millions of people from all walks of life throughout the world. This can happen to anyone. There is no discrimination against anxiety. When stress grows in us, it can cause symptoms of physical suffering, which can be a terrible thing.

The symptoms of an anxiety attack can make you think you have a heart attack, stroke, or other serious medical emergencies. As a result, most people who suffer from anxiety rush to the emergency room to determine that their condition is not life-threatening.

Anxiety attacks start suddenly in most people and last about 10 minutes. However, in some cases, they can take an hour or more. A seizure is a feeling of intense anxiety, horror, and sudden discomfort. Anxiety can occur at any time, even while sleeping.

The most common symptoms of an anxiety attack are discomfort or anxiety of difficulty breathing. A strong desire to run or escape from a place where you have trouble swallowing your chest or heart palpitations or trembling weak or slow sweat or numb feet.

Anxiety attacks are like a false alarm of our brain on our bodies. When we are in real danger, our body's fight or flight mechanism is activated to protect us from danger. When we see signs of anxiety, we feel the same waves of anxiety and horror, all the physical effects that accompany them, like a heart beating fast.

The difference between panic attacks and anxiety is that with anxiety, there is no immediate threat.

Anxiety can occur without treatment and form a tendency that can cause anxiety disorders. One of the worst symptoms of anxiety is an increase in anxiety when and where the next anxiety disorder will occur. This option often causes more dangerous attacks. It can be a painful cycle of doubt and uncertainty.

What can be done to treat the symptoms of anxiety attacks?

The good news is that depression is a very curable condition. There are many ways to deal with anxiety attacks. The most common are psychotherapy, medication (antidepressants or natural herbal treatments), and cognitive therapy. At least two of these strategies have proven to be the most successful combinations.

Doctors recommend using antidepressants in almost every situation to help combat anxiety disorders. The use of antidepressants, including addictions and severe side effects, is dangerous.

However, new research shows that antidepressants do not work in nearly half of all anxiety disorders. This is a scary figure. Based on these facts, the decision not to take mild antidepressants should not be made. This finding has recently led to an increase in the market for alternative treatments for natural anxiety.

So what should you do?

The most important fact that you must understand if you suffer from this disease is that anxiety attacks cannot harm you. What you need is Time! It is essential to understand this. Most people, especially those who are just scared, start to think of all the bad things that can happen during an anxiety attack and worsen the signs.

Begin your recovery by taking the time to realize what anxiety is and how to deal with it. Once you understand the truth of this disorder, start exercising to treat the signs of anxiety attacks that you encounter.

Practice various behavioural strategies during and during an anxiety attack. This includes, but is not limited to, calming, breathing techniques, visualization, and cognitive reprogramming. Look for support groups online or directly in various depression forums.

Look for high-quality natural remedies for depression before you become more dangerous and addictive. You may need to argue with a doctor, but this is your decision. Natural alternatives are less damaging, far safer, and in many cases, act as antidepressants.

The result is acting. Don't allow yourself to sit still with signs of anxiety. If you find that you cannot take action on your own, contact your family or doctor.

Now stop the nightmare anxiety attack before it gets worse. The more you participate in recovery and rehabilitation, the faster you take control of your life.

CHAPTER TWO

ANXIETY DISORDERS

Anxiety is a term used for various disorders that can cause intense physical symptoms, nervousness, and anxiety. Various anxiety states cause mental and physical health problems and which can interfere with more severe symptoms. Anxiety usually arises when you are faced with something outside your comfort zone and with it many stressful situations. For example, if you want to take a test, take an interview, or talk.

This affects people differently because this situation might be considered normal for some people, but they can change your entire life, such as B. Sleeping, mistakes at work, or the inability to eat properly. In general, anxiety arises when an excessive response is expected. Anxiety disorders can be divided into certain types. The most common form of anxiety is below:

General A.D

Depression is defined as constant long-term anxiety and anxiety of unknown events and circumstances. This GAD Those who worry about the problem. This can be family life, work challenges, security, and money, but it can be challenging to control your anxiety. Outsiders often find this anxiety rather trivial and overwhelmed by what is usually expected of this situation. This can sometimes seem unwise because it might be challenging to focus on someone who has small but tricky everyday problems such as social activities, relationships, and work-related issues.

Post-traumatic stress disorder (PTSD) is a depression caused by a very stressful event from the previous situation. This can be a severe case as if someone has been mistreated or involved in a severe incident such as hostage-taking, rape, or war. Post-traumatic stress disorder includes side effects and can trigger stressful behaviour when a situation is called upon.

What is intrusive OCD?

Obsessive Compulsive Disorder (OCD) is an anxiety disorder that can be excessive and repetitive. However, customers reduce their intrusive frustrations by focusing on specific models, e.g., B. compulsive hand washing, testing door locks, replacing oven lamps, and cleaning personal items without end.

Social anxiety disorder is a social phobia for public humiliation and is considered a negative attitude. Social anxiety disorder examples are anxiety of intimacy or when the artist is very depressed by stage anxiety. This can have a severe impact on victims by being lonely and avoiding the appearance of living conditions in public, which makes healthy life almost impossible.

Panic disorder is a type of disease that is defined as a short and fast episode of intense anxiety, and that causes breathing problems, dizziness, and nausea.

After 15 minutes, anxiety attacks can begin and peak very quickly, but last for hours. Anxiety disorders often occur after a traumatic encounter or chronic stress, but can also occur spontaneously. Anxiety attacks can remind a person of changes in normal bodily functions, which can be interpreted as life-threatening hypervigilance symptoms associated with hypochondria. It can cause other annoying attacks that can cause dramatic changes in behaviour to stop the attack.

What is Phobia?

A phobia is indescribable anxiety of an entity, event, or situation that leads to panic or an uncontrolled response that makes it very difficult to control behaviour. In general, many people have a phobia, and it's easy for them to avoid this situation, but those who, in many cases, are involved in their phobia immediately change their behaviour, and they have to run away.

What is an anxiety disorder?

Separation Anxiety disorder is a condition where someone with anxiety and irrational behaviour is far from a particular object, person, or place. In particular, it is difficult to deal with new environments when people leave home or when families are separated, which leads to excessive or inappropriate behaviour.

Symptoms of depression? People with anxiety disorders have many different physical and non-physical symptoms, such as intense and absurd anxiety that is characterized by the disease. Many of these symptoms are similar to people with a common condition, heart attack, or stroke, and this leads to an increase in additional anxiety.

The list of physical symptoms related to generalized anxiety disorder, sleep disorders includes Lighter muscle tension, anxiety headaches, stomach fatigue, vomiting of pins, and needles.

Panic patients may experience physical symptoms similar to those with a generalized anxiety disorder. You may also experience shortness of breath, convulsions, and feelings of shock.

Various symptoms of post-traumatic stress disorder only occur with this form of anxiety. More extreme symptomatic behaviour, hallucinations or trauma that re-experiment, avoiding people, difficulty concentrating, inability to sleep well while watching the environment (hyper-vigilance), feeling of lack or annoyance or future aspirations.

Other factors such as medication, brain disorders, genetics, early childhood experiences, and a combination of these. The most common depression is tension in our lives and lack of trust when others around them succeed.

Internal and social causes

Environmental factors that cause various types of anxiety are known, including injuries caused by incidents such as death, violence, psychological or physical, or victimization of relatives or relatives. Stress in personal contact, marriage, friendship Stress at work in schools, colleges, or universities Stress related to money and financial problems, lack of oxygen in high places.

Health Causes Depression is associated with health factors such as anaemia, asthma, infections, and various cardiovascular diseases. There are several causes of clinical anxiety, such as signs of a condition or medical procedure, side effects of treatment, lack of pulmonary embolism or emphysema, drug use, and violence.

With some anxiety disorders such as panic disorder, social phobia, or general anxiety disorder, many people who are addicted to alcohol or drugs suffer from mental health problems.

The result is more common anxiety: an overdose of drugs such as amphetamine or cocaine or when someone stops using illegal drugs such as heroin or prescription drugs such as Vicodin, barbiturates, or benzodiazepines.

Genetics

The most unfortunate reason is that if the family has been afraid in the past, it is possible to develop. Some people have a tendency towards genetics, which gives them a higher chance of anxiety.

Brain chemistry researchers have found that people with elevated levels of certain neurotransmitters in their brains are more likely to suffer from a generalized anxiety disorder.

When neurotransmitters do not function properly, the brain's internal communication network dissolves, and in certain situations, the brain can work incorrectly and differently. And this can cause anxiety.

BENEFITS OF HAVING ANXIETY

The truth you need to know is that those who learn to live with it and face the challenge of not letting go of their anxieties will eventually have several "fins" that offer unexpected benefits overall ordinary people who have never had to face them every day of the worst anxieties.

There are many explanations for why anxiety can occur, some are even hereditary, and are entirely independent of environmental factors, but for many of us, anxiety is an unconscious way of telling us that something is wrong, although we may not have a clue at that time.

Before the anxiety and terrible stress that can be caused by anxiety, we can have one of the worst experiences in life, but over time (and sometimes it takes a long time, which is good). You see trends in your anxiety or symptoms.

I have been there. I still have a long way to go. Apparently, without controlling my anxiety, including several sessions with different therapists trying to find my anxiety, it usually doesn't work.

It seemed to me that my life was great - I played everything negative and frustrating, and I convinced myself that I was happy, even if a part of me said no. Only after years of anxiety, I was allowed to accept that the real things in my life scared me or even felt real physical symptoms and that I did not communicate with myself.

In retrospect, it's hard to believe that I couldn't see how depressed I was and how I didn't allow myself to pursue my passions, but that was a blind spot for me at that time.

Now I'm not saying you do the same thing, but anxiety is a challenging journey that brings a reward that is useful when you begin to feel the victory over your anxiety. You start to realize that you have to listen to what you want, and you can find your true identity and make calls in life only when you learn not to let your anxiety decide for you.

New motivation and goals

The constant struggle against anxiety compels a person to develop strong core values and the drive to do meaningful things in one's life - one can even say that anxiety is a jerk from one's own life that keeps him away from his emotions and keep mentally awkward.

Anxiety immediately takes us away from our comfort zone, and we are forced to struggle to live at a far more difficult level, which can cause you to refrain from rethinking all your life choices and the current goals that you want (or) to achieve).

I have a complicated way of understanding that I don't have to follow the path of others or encourage my hopes to please others. I find my passion for things that interest me and ultimately get rid of the emotions I'm worried about if I can't publish the picture that I made in my head.

It gives me new and useful motivation and gives me new strength to pursue goals that inspire me actively every day. And even though anxiety never disappears entirely and appears in the corners of your mind, anxiety slowly loses its influence on your feelings when you find happiness in the things you seek. In my opinion, reading is a must because it contains some basic psychological thoughts of self-awareness and clear instructions on how to change it for the better.

It gives you courage and self-confidence, not something provided only for those who are afraid or panicked - this is an integral part of human experience. Hell is an integral part of the experience of almost all living things. Anxiety prevents people from being erased from this earth in the earliest morning of our existence, and it plays a vital role in our civilization today.

On the other hand, anxiety is what prevents many people from returning to life - even if the anxiety is very subtle and penetrates their minds, you can still hesitate to try anything to achieve your real dream, or even ask people who like that day.

However, if you experience "pleasure" developing anxiety disorders and/or anxiety attacks, along with evident paralysis that can cause you to stop functioning normally, your mood will change. If you succeed in getting out and out of the other party, this can give you a new feeling of courage and confidence.

Even everyday situations that usually stress people can be far less frightening if you manage to control your anxiety: public speaking, interviews, big tests, all pale compared to full-blown anxiety attacks that might be caused by your efforts to overcome anxiety more relaxed than most people.

You may know that anxiety attacks are misinterpretations of our body and fight or flight responses that aim to prepare our bodies for extreme situations such as fighting, fleeing, or dealing with large mountain lions.

Even though this is a challenge, if you are not in real danger because of the bewildering effect of a sizzling heart, a throbbing mind, dizziness, and many more that are triggered by the release of adrenaline and other chemicals from our brain, there are several benefits - if you continue to get to exposed continuously to threats (but not in real danger), the mind will get used to these sensations.

You are forced to go through daily life, sometimes experience this ANXIETY, and inevitably learn to deal with it and function normally. And that means that even when it's very urgent, you can keep your mind relatively calm and not be able to lose it completely.

Some therapists who experience anxiety and panic prepare you for extreme situations in your life - your body, is "so trained" to fight or run away that you won't get angry if a crisis happens because other people can react faster and make rational decisions while others freeze up.

While it is good to have an "advantage" in extreme situations, the reality is that most of us may be happy to avoid such situations altogether.

Although you may remain as calm as Samuel L. Jackson in dealing with real-life situations that threaten your own or someone else's life, you agree that it's better to avoid such situations and save yourself from the hassles.

The good news is that while anxiety pushes us to avoid social situations and even activities that we like because of anxiety, which is not is not fun at all; it can also help us develop habits, rationally assess situations, and calculate risks before we decide. Even if you overcome your first anxiety and return to a relatively normal life, you can measure potential hazards almost compulsively but effectively in different scenarios.

However, you can't think of it as a threat instead of "feeling scared or vulnerable" when walking down a dark alley with your girlfriend, walking into a shady alley, or even driving after drinking.

Although some people might argue that Yolo (or what children call it now, I'm getting older) is so charming that you can make sensible and rational decisions, at least giving you a better chance to live long enough (if you want) or at least find out what happened in the last Game of Thrones.

It's hard to ignore something unpleasant like anxiety disorders - it's a terrible experience for millions of people around the world, so there's no reason why it's "healthy" at all. But it is important to find the point of light even in our toughest battles like anxiety, because if you see it as an experience, you will find that your struggle against anxiety has made you stronger. You can be proud of the types of difficulties you have to face every day and believe in all areas of life. And whether you are having a "bad day" or on your way to recovery, remember that the same depression that seems to take your life will make you live your life to the full.

LIFESTYLE FACTORS THAT CAN BE ADDED BECAUSE OF ANXIETY

If you don't have anxiety for a long time, Behaviour change will take time for someone to recover from anxiety. You must also act during this recovery phase concerned. (Behaviour change) and maintain confidence in the process.

Returns and relapses occur if a change in behaviour is not held for a reasonable time to recover. This is often because the process of anxiety and recovery is not fully understood and that additional life factors hinder the recovery process.

Lifestyle factors that can cause depression are:

> **You consume too much caffeine**

Coffee is associated with increased anxiety. When dealing with chronic anxiety, try to reduce all caffeine and caffeine products. If you find this very difficult, try limiting your intake and gradually limiting yourself. Because caffeine leaves your system, caffeine has a positive effect on your nervous system.

➢ You don't exercise enough

Staying active is important to reduce stress and anxiety. Please note that the term "sports" does not mean that marathons must be practised. Best of all, this is a nice little road down the road. Go to sports today and soon you will develop new habits and feel good.

➢ You don't have to sleep

This is one of the main reasons and is often associated with too much coffee. Anxiety and depression are associated with constant sleep deprivation.Remember the importance of rest as food and exercise.

➢ You drink too much alcohol

Don't get me wrong, but what happens to our bodies when we drink? A glass of random wine doesn't hurt me? Well, alcohol is a poison that can contribute to mental and physical abuse by affecting the level of serotonin in the brain (a factor that feels good).

When someone is anxious and stressed, the man's anxieties can make him feel worse and cause more symptoms.

➢ **You have no place to relax or deal with stress**

It's essential to see how you deal with stress/anxiety in life. Too much thinking about the past and/or future would trigger anxiety. Meditation often helps us to stay in a time when there is no depression. Even 10 minutes a day can have a positive impact on your overall health. As Tony Robbins said, "If you don't have ten minutes a day, you don't have a life!"

➢ **Eat a balanced diet**

Blueberries, asparagus, milk, almonds and spinach are reported to be reduced. Avoid beer, chocolate, fried foods, processed foods, and refined sugar at all costs. Most say that if you eat lots of fruits and vegetables and healthy foods above, you will feel the best and most comfortable.

➢ You don't have enough friends and bad relationships

This is the perfect way to feel happier and less stressed with strong social networks. It's good to have friends at work too. We spend so much time at work and must build positive relationships that are good for our well-being. If we accept that we are angry or upset with people in our lives, our attitude and well-being, in general, will be affected. The same thing applies to relationships with families.

➢ Don't have fun

When we make contact and have fun, it considers our thoughts and anxieties and gives our body and mind plenty of time to relax. The explanation for this is that if your mind does not stop at the perceived threat, it does not cause a stress response.

When you focus on things that aren't nervous, your mind and body begin to relax and relax. People often say how happy they are after an exciting day full of friends and family. Time to enjoy and balance work is one of the most important things to achieve psychological well-being.

> **You work too hard**

For many people, their work is the most stressful in their lives. Even though most of us can't control everything in the workplace, it's essential for us to focus on what we can control. When your workday is over, let it stop! Don't bring your work problems into your personal life as often as possible.

Your depression should not be treated at the expense of your well-being or your spouse's well-being. Choose a trusted doctor who can help you find a strategy if you need to talk about work problems.

> **You eat too much sugar**

Most of us have heard that too much sugar is bad for us, but do we know why? Studies show that too much sugar raises the risk of heart disease. The effect of sugar has been linked to solid drugs in other studies.

Sugar also creates a rapid burst of energy, followed by interference - similar to caffeine. It stimulates adrenaline and cortisol in your body and can cause increased anxiety and panic. I prefer to eat authentic food.

How can you benefit from attention and relaxation?

Learning to relax is needed to stay calm. Regular breaks throughout the day have been proven to relieve anxiety and help clarify stressful thoughts. Relaxation techniques that are practised often stimulate the body's normal soothing response (deep resting state) compared to the stress response felt when our body is travelling or struggling with stress. The relaxation reaction slows down stress and restores the balance between body and mind.

Meditation or "caution" has repeatedly shown positive effects on overcoming anxiety. Even though it does not dispel anxiety itself, it is a practice that has a positive impact on your emotional health. Some advantages are explained below.

> **Overcoming stress**

Studies show that constant awareness increases positive emotions and reduces stress/anxiety. The more you meditate, the more brain structure changes, releasing anti-stress chemicals that eliminates anxiety.

Aside from this daily perception, it also increases your ability to deal with stress, ensuring that no event ever worries you.

➢ **Better sleep**

Meditation improves sleep quality when done regularly. This has a very positive effect on reducing overused thoughts. The more you rest, your body becomes calmer.

Remember that rest is a natural way of relieving stress and anxiety. In contrast to these findings, routine perceptions have shown that high neurochemical melatonin is used in sleep.

An accelerated thought that does not disappear is a common symptom of anxiety. Through regular meditation, you can learn to break away from these thoughts and concentrate on your inner silence. The more you meditate, the better you deviate from disturbing thoughts when you return to this place.

CHAPTER THREE

DESTRUCTIVE ANXIETY DISORDERS AND SYMPTOMS

Almost everyone feels anxious, nervous, afraid, worried, or panicked. The colloquial term is anxiety, and this experience is entirely normal. However, this training is important to what extent and to what extent you have overcome it. Because anxiety can cause anxiety attacks and is associated with many threats to life and phobias. There are 14 major anxiety disorders and signs that can damage your life and your family. For example, most children are afraid of darkness. Failure to cope with the condition of early childhood can lead to the possibility of phobias.

There are millions of people today who hate darkness and cannot sleep at night. You have to wait for the sun to rise before you can relax. However, if a child or even an adult is informed and respected and knows that there is nothing to anxiety, the problem is resolved.

Anxiety can be represented in many ways. Webster described anxiety as distress or discomfort caused by anxiety of danger or misery. Research shows that anxiety can also be an emotional response to the use of criticism or excessive judgment.

Other sources describe anxiety as a normal stress response; This inherent strength helps us deal with stressful situations at home and work. This provides a mechanism by which we can focus on competitive events and can make efforts to study hard for important exams.

However, depression helps us deal with situations. But the question is, "Do you just want to face it?" This can cause serious injury. Medical research shows that depression is associated with high blood pressure and many other diseases. You see, there are many aspects of anxiety.

Although it is associated with high blood pressure, it also protects you from real dangers and promotes growth and change. Also, it is a medical fact that some anxiety is natural. However, if you continually respond to circumstances that are not a real threat, that anxiety becomes insufficient.

Feeling

Anxiety occurs in many ways, such as panic, anxiety, horror, anxiety, anger, sadness, and anxiety. Medical symptoms may include dizziness, fatigue, heartbeat, sweating, numbness, cold or sticky hands, shortness of breath, diarrhoea, numbness, numbness, weakness, pressure and redness.

Anxiety can strike or roll like lightning. This can be characterized by constant anxiety and chaos. It can also be a natural anxiety associated with life challenges and minor difficulties such as losing a job, crashing a car, or having a serious illness. Is not unexpected or direct

Respond to big threats, emotions and similar physical anxieties. The feeling of panic is caused by an overreaction in the first phase of the body's stress response, commonly referred to as a fight or run response. Moderate to mild anxiety can be a bit excessive and more serious.

However, if you experience this feeling of inadequate anxiety or constant worry, you are not alone. Do not worry; it can happen. The good news is that you don't have to suffer all the time.

Here are some anxiety issues related to anxiety that you might not know about: Anxiety in its various forms - anxiety, muscle aches, pain, rapid shallow breathing, fatigue, palpitations, headaches - is one of the most common complaints that heard by a doctor. Alcoholism, irritable bowel syndrome, premenstrual syndrome and many other medical problems can be caused or worsened by anxiety.

> More than twice as many women as restless men. It is unknown whether this is because women care more or men tend to resist anxiety.
> There are signs of depression every year in 65 million Americans, 30 million of whom are seriously ill.
> One in two in the United States suffers from mild to moderate anxiety for at least two weeks, with one in four suffering from anxiety disorders.
> According to a recent survey, more than 25 per cent of the US population suffers from chronic anxiety and stress.

Although more people are afraid than other mental health problems, less than 25 per cent receive adequate support. This means that around 18 million people now suffer from a disease that cannot be treated.

This is a list of major anxiety disorders and their symptoms that affect millions of people around the world every day:

1. Most Damaging Anxiety Disorders and Anxiety Attack Symptoms:

This person suddenly feels that they will go crazy, die, or lose control. PD (panic disorder) is called this type of disorder.

2. Force:

This type of person must perform rituals such as counting objects, washing objects repeatedly, praying, arranging things in certain ways, or repeating words quietly. Another form of this condition is called OCD. OBS.

3. Concerns about your appearance:

This type of person believes that their appearance is abnormal or strange, even if no one can see the defect.

BDD (Dysmorphic Body Disturbance) is this type of disorder.

4. Other types of people have annoying ideas that they cannot get rid of, such as anxiety of losing control and hurting others, acknowledging that they have not committed a crime or are contaminated with dust or germs. Intrusiveness: The word OCD (Obsessive Compulsive Disorder) indicates this form of the disorder.

5. Chronic ANXIETY:

People like this are always worried about work, family, health, school or finance. GAD (Generalized Anxiety Disorder) is a type of disease.

6. ANXIETY Test:

This type of person becomes nervous and freezes when tests are needed. SAA (Social Anxiety Disorder) is considered this type of disorder.

7. Agoraphobia:

This person is afraid that something bad will happen if they are away from home alone. This type of disease is called agoraphobia (agoraphobia).

8. Concerns about public speaking:

Talking to a group of people bothers them. This disease is a type of SAD (Social Anxiety Disorder).

9. ANXIETY and phobias:

This type of person is very afraid of certain things like flying, driving, turning, blood, high altitude or stranded in a smaller place. This is known as this type of disorder (specific phobia).

10. Health problems:

These people often worry about serious medical problems or illnesses, even if doctors often tell him that everything is fine. This is called this type of disorder (hypochondria).

11. Shame:

This type of person often feels nervous or aware of other people. This type of SAD (social anxiety disorder) is considered a form of this disorder.

12. Shy Bladder Syndrome:

This person is worried about using public toilets. Social anxiety disorder is seen as a manifestation of this type of disorder.

13. Post-traumatic stress disorder:

This type of person is haunted by trauma-anxiety memories, including death, harassment, harassment, serious injury or torture. This list of signs and anxiety disorders is compiled by a group of doctors who meet annually to vote on the latest version of their diagnostic criteria.

Please note, however, that marking such conditions does not 100% place the person in a particular disorder category. Most doctors find it somewhat unclear and misleading to mention the disease. However, this is an industry-standard.

Research has shown that anxiety is associated with a variety of mental and physical disorders that can sometimes be fatal. Research also shows that anxiety is normal; It protects us from real danger and drives growth and change.

To avoid the depression that is full of anxiety, regular exercise, yoga, golf, and meditation can be a good platform for a calm mind. Only if you go out for a few minutes every morning and meditate to rest instead of continuing negative events, you will live a new life full of optimism, not filled with anxiety, insecurity and anxiety.

If you create a harmonious and prosperous world, depression has no entry point other than terror and insecurity. Remember that anxiety and calm cannot occupy the same room at the same time.

HOW TO STOP ANXIETY ATTACKS - NOT JUST MANAGE THEM

Specific concepts such as togetherness; Interaction; Community members; Friend; be accepted; friendly and kind; Open yourself to others etc. They are relating to personal words and culture.

Nearly every aspect of our lives is about circumstances in which we "present" something - where we need to "relate" to other people, where we are evaluated, measured, judged, rejected, approved, praised or ridiculed.

An anxious adult who wonders how to avoid anxiety attacks to destroy their lives, anticipate and experience debilitating social anxieties when they must participate in the most non-threatening social events.

One explanation for the enormous anxiety in our society is a fundamental change in our culture. Where family life used to be combined and put together, we now have families in one place, isolated from relatives, grandparents in other places, and young people in other places.

A sense of identity, ownership, and security that is "combined" with current absence and anxiety disorders is widespread. There is a great need to cure how anxiety attacks can be stopped.

People affected by social anxiety will do everything possible to prevent situations and opportunities to reach others because they cannot control their suffering in a social context.

In addition to identifying the cause of anxiety, most anxiety attack treatments focus on this side of the disorder. Therapy centres also recognize that alcohol is often a self-managed analgesic - a source of anxiety management.

When we discuss some of the underlying data, it's time to focus on symptoms and treatment of social anxiety. Perhaps the two physical signs that suffer the most and suffer the most are redness or redness and tremor.

Certain physical symptoms of chest pain, palpitations, sudden extremes, and dry mouth contrast with the psychic manifestations of persistent and disappearing anxieties and worries about problems that do not appeal to others.

Maybe family members who have never fully understood the extraordinary need to avoid anxiety attacks on one of their relatives will now show more compassion and work harder to find the right procedure.

Fortunately, various treatments are available, including social anxiety, to avoid anxiety attacks. Medications such as antidepressants and betting blockers, like all anxiety medications, can be offered by doctors for symptom management, but they cannot claim to provide drugs to prevent anxiety attacks - they cannot claim treatment.

The solution is that the unconscious practice of keeping anxiety alive has been discovered and eliminated. This special treatment, which focuses on avoiding anxiety attacks, especially social anxiety, is mental, which means dealing with, influencing, and primarily acting as awareness and motivation.

There are therapies specifically designed to treat problems, including CBT, cognitive-behavioural therapy, and Linden's treatment method. The purpose of CBT in treating social anxiety is to prepare someone to find patterns of thought and action, and then to confront and question them.

This allows the patient to understand the cause of his anxiety, to learn, to adjust his thought patterns and behaviour through anxiety counselling and to follow the process consistently. You have a personal responsibility to learn how to stop attacks that interfere with your life.

How to treat anxiety disorders, especially how to avoid anxiety attacks instead of feeling all the signs and pain directly. And now there is a cure for social anxiety that not only reduces symptoms but also cures all types of anxiety disorders.

THE BASICS OF ANTI-DISEASE CARE

It is crucial for you to know that if the ability to attend certain events or locations prevents you from constantly being afraid of things that can happen, many feel satisfied instead of living their lives. Patients with anxiety disorders may think that their "illness" is out of control, but it may not be far from the truth.

Sufferers can accept their symptoms with appropriate forms of treatment for anxiety disorders because this is a condition that causes people to be physically, psychologically, emotionally, or spiritually scared or disturbed in various situations and not illness.

In this case, a person's normal ANXIETY s become a nuisance because the mind and body can no longer respond to situations normally. Regardless of how bad your symptoms are, you can use the right help and support to treat anxiety disorders.

Some people might choose to use drugs to relieve their anxiety symptoms, and while some might work, it might not be the only healthy lifestyle decision. Although some people may argue differently, drugs have a very low success rate in treating the symptoms of anxiety disorders that do not give good results for long-term success in controlling your anxiety.

Anxiety disorders affect those who choose treatment and usually take medicine for a while, producing a kind of yo-yo effect that is repeated without resolving this problem forever. The symptoms tend to keep the patient from returning to the life he once loved until the underlying causes of his depression are discussed.

Based on extensive research, it has been determined that the most effective treatment for anxiety disorders is to combine the right type of self-help with the help of a qualified therapist who specializes in restoring anxiety.

A coach, counsellor, therapist, or even a psychologist who has overcome anxiety and has been drug-free for at least three years is all good to choose the right therapist for anxiety disorders.

Therapists who are taking medication to overcome their problems have shown that they are not good medicine for anxiety. Studies show that those who work with therapists who have anxiety disorders are the best helpers to deal with their unique forms. Those who are still on anxiety drugs may wonder how helpful the therapist is if they cannot overcome their anxiety disorder.

Despite this claim that some psychiatric professionals experience interference, experience shows that this statement is generally true. Many of you who previously asked one of these specialists to assist in the treatment of anxiety disorders find that your condition continues or even worsens after diagnosis.

Anxiety disorders can be treated, but you need the right information and support to stop your anxiety disorders forever. There are two classes of anxiety disorder:

General Anxiety: This form of anxiety disorder is often characterized by symptoms caused by acute stress, condition, or emotions. For example, relationship problems, professional challenges, illness, death of a loved one, or even academic pressure can cause but are not limited to, a constant level of anxiety.

Because stress accumulation often precedes anxiety, most forms of early stress can be divided into this group. After a stressful event, state or even emotions are finished, the use of appropriate ingredients, rest and time help the patient to decide his anxieties.

Chronic anxiety: This type of anxiety is usually characterized by symptoms that occur for several months to a year or more and then disappear.

Examples are people with symptoms that appear and appear at various stages of their lives. As a rule, symptoms persist as a continuing background to their lives, and these symptoms are usually turned on and off throughout their lives unless they are treated properly for anxiety disorders.

A predictable form of panic or anxiety that can occur because you are worried or afraid that something will happen. The kind of unintentional anxiety or panic that can appear alone or in blue. Situational anxiety or even sudden predictions are usually not the results of this form of anxiety or panic.

It is a good idea to be help by someone who has lived and overcome the same level of anxiety in their own life in terms of treating anxiety disorders. The experience they make will significantly contribute to your recovery.

If you know that you are not depressed, it will immediately seem easier to find the right solution than you ever imagined.

CHAPTER FOUR

IMMEDIATE ANTIQUITY - NATURAL MECHANISM FOR FAST SERIES AND ASCETIC ATTACKS FAST!

His anxiety was too great, so he missed the first day of class T, so he didn't have to go to class. Anxiety is the way your body tells you to act against threats or dangerous situation.

Therefore, anxiety can be beneficial or constructive when asked to take appropriate action in response to anxiety. The worst of all feelings is undoubtedly anxiety. Not only experienced by all humans, but an alarming reaction is also found in all animal species, even in sea slugs. Anxiety is almost always caused by exposure to anxious social situations, even panic attacks, even though anxiety is considered excessive and unreasonable.

This belief can lead to avoidance or perseverance in extreme suffering, which leads to a significant decline in individual functions and routines. If your anxiety is an individual response - for example, a blow given to you by a doctor - your anxiety will decrease, and your symptoms will disappear after the incident.

If you are divided between your mother-in-law and your anxieties, you will likely be afraid for a while before and after you see it. If you live, the costs of depression are unclear. This uncertainty can cost tens of thousands of dollars during your career.

However, the cause of depression is still unclear. This is associated with a poor response to psychostimulant therapy, and alternative pharmacotherapy methods are suggested. Anxiety is often associated with physical and behavioural changes, such as anxiety. Anxiety is not a common stress response, but stress can cause anxiety if it lasts long enough. There are many types of stress in our lives, many of which are inevitable.

The most effective way to overcome anxiety is to change anxiety into mental anxiety. Then you know what exactly is bothering you. anxiety is a problem when our body reacts as if there is no real danger.

It's like a smoker alarm device that is too weak for your skin! Studies show that general anxiety can be adequately controlled and managed for three to four months when the person is empowered and works to recover.

For anxiety of negative feedback, it's controversial whether the anxiety test itself is a real anxiety disorder or whether it's a special type of social phobia. The anxiety of this test is not caused by the test, but by the importance of the person attached to the test.

If you tell yourself that you are not doing well or you are not exercising enough, you have an emotional response that is compatible with this text. Anxiety is a cross-system response to perceived threats. It is a mixture of physiological changes in the body, the past and memory of people and social situations.

Anxiety is an emotion that sends our thoughts into the future. After all, nobody worries about the past, right? As a former patient, I know what depression is and how it can interfere with normal life. I know that treating depression does not require addictive drugs. The way you think and behave responsibly to make you worry about performance.

However, many parents don't seek treatment because they think anxiety is normal, and this is a lifetime, that is part of me. "Anxiety of execution is often seen as anxiety of public speaking.

However, people whose jobs or other interests allow them to "step on stage" for other reasons, like actor, singer, athlete, etc., considered as a stage problem as a limitation of their activities.

Anxiety is a common condition that occurs for no apparent reason. As such, it ranges from anxiety to the presence of perceived threats. It is essential to understand the difference between heart attack and anxiety. As a heart attack, many people are suspected of being afraid. It is normal to be afraid of big events. If anxiety is a constant problem in your life, plan to talk to someone regularly every week.

The physiological arousal that we experience as anxiety is directly related to the anxiety of danger. We react psychologically and physically when we risk our physical well-being, which can result in serious physical injury or death. Anxiety is a natural response to stress.

This allows you to deal with stressful situations at work, make interviews more difficult to research and concentrate on important speeches. One way to overcome anxiety is to develop a passive attitude. This might work, but patience and patience are needed.

Anxiety is feeling nervous, afraid, or worried. Many anxieties and worries are justified, e.g. For example, worrying about a loved one, or taking an exam. The word social anxiety is often used for feelings such as shame and shame.

However, some psychologists distinguish between different types of social discomfort and determine criteria for anxiety. For me, the problem is a list of suggestions and suggestions sent when I have time. However, you can use it for all types of charts.

Anxiety is an uncomfortable feeling that can allows us to get out of dangerous situations, make us worry and motivate us to face problems. Too little depression is based on satisfaction on the other side of the spectrum. If we are not too afraid, we avoid change, respect the status quo and believe that everything will be okay.

Depression is a disorder that grows throughout our culture. Medications to treat moderate to mild anxiety, especially benzodiazepines, are dangerous because they can cause injury, side effects, and addiction. Anyone except anxiety is permitted during the interview.

Spots of laughter and tears come out, but when people are nervous, which usually causes hyperventilation, they stop and breathe. Anxiety is usually caused by a situation that involves a decision or judgment; Learning exams and assessments are a common sign of anxiety.

Some have vague feelings of anxiety that never reach the intensity of panic attacks. When artists are on stage, their anxieties are focused on concentrated energy. Practice the test with your research team and be safer during the test.

OVERCOMING ANXIETY?

Anxiety disorders can cause problems in your daily life, especially in your daily activities and relationships. Therefore, it's best to deal with anxiety and treat your anxiety disorder as quickly and efficiently as possible to come back to life before the anxiety disorder develops. There are several methods that you can use to overcome your anxiety. The self-help approach is one possibility.

For some people, self-help strategies are enough to overcome anxiety. However, it is important to note that self-help strategies only reduce your anxiety and do not overcome the root cause of your anxiety.

Some effective self-help techniques for dealing with anxiety include: becoming more productive with anxiety - this includes triggering irrational anxiety thinking, studying delays in care, and learning to live unsafe lives.

Make the lifestyle changes needed to reduce anxiety. This means you can get rid of caffeine, start exercising, strengthen your health, and benefit from the help of your family and friends.

Techniques for learning and practising relaxation - deep breathing and awareness. When the ability to relax improves, the nervous system becomes less sensitive and less susceptible to stress and anxiety.

Knowing how to relax is another effective way to deal with anxiety. Most people with anxiety disorders cannot relax and control themselves. Learning how to do it is easy, and the ability to overcome anxiety will make a big difference. One or more physical senses, the senses of sight, sound, smell, touch, and taste, are the best methods for self-control.

Spectacle: Enjoy the beautiful scenery, take a walk in a beautiful area, admire art in an art museum or explore an interesting photo book.

Sound - Hear Soothing Music Relax in nature, like singing birds or crashing into the ocean waves on the beach.

Smooth, light scented candles, smell natural flowers, breathe clean, smooth air, or spray your favourite scent. Touch your cat or dog, wash warm, cover with a soft blanket, feel the cool breeze or massage.

Tastefully - Prepare delicious food, slowly enjoy your favourite handwriting or drink a cup of coffee, tea or chocolate.

Self-help strategies are not enough for certain people to deal with depression. Anxiety still prevented him from living his life. This is the time to seek professional help to overcome depression. You should consult with a psychologist to ensure that your anxiety disorder is common because new symptoms or traumatic events can cause problems other than general anxiety.

Depression, substance abuse, and other anxiety disorders can also be associated with a generalized anxiety disorder. Overcoming depression means treating all your symptoms, not just a few.

The best way to deal with depression is to use self-help strategies and advice. Therapy not only can help you deal with depression but also has no side effects. Cognitive separation therapy is an effective therapy for overcoming anxiety caused by a widespread anxiety disorder.

Cognitive-behavioural therapy involves dealing with differences in the way we see the environment and ourselves. Cognitive-behavioural therapy allows you to identify negative thoughts and resolve those anxieties automatically.

Cognitive behavioural treatment consists of five main components: Training that helps you understand more about your depression and distinguish between useful and useless problems.

Observation: You will learn what triggers your anxiety, what specific things you are worried about, how difficult, and how long a particular episode lasts.

Physical Control Strategies - Deep breathing and progressive muscle relaxation can reduce your "opponent or run" response which maintains your anxiety and anxiety.

Cognitive Management Techniques - You can reduce your anxieties and start solving anxieties by learning to assess objectively and change thinking habits that lead to generalized anxiety disorder.

Station strategy - You will feel more in control and less anxious if you confront your anxieties directly without trying to avoid them.

In extreme cases of generalized anxiety disorder, medication can be used temporarily. Three main types of drugs used to treat generalized anxiety disorders include buspirone, the safest drug for dealing with anxiety. It just takes the edge and doesn't eliminate anxiety.

Benzodiazepines - These drugs work very fast (usually within 30 to 60 minutes), but can be physically and mentally addictive if taken within a few weeks.

Antidepressants - It takes six weeks for this drug to be effective. They can affect the quality of sleep and make some patients feel sick.

When you ask for professional help and make a medical assessment, you can decide if you have an anxiety disorder and how best to treat it.

ANXIETY MEDICATIONS

Most doctors prescribe medications to treat some symptoms and work through counselling. However, there is information about anxiety medications that patients need to know before taking them.

The question that people should ask about anxiety medications is whether they can save lives. The following are some common issues that can give patients valuable insight and information about treatment for anxiety. Your doctor should ask you the following questions about certain medicines prescribed: What type of medication is prescribed for you?

It is essential for patients to know what drugs to take and whether to prescribe generic alternatives or not.

How many times a day do I have to take the right dose?

Information about this anxiety treatment can affect or affect your ability to function. With certain medicines, you must take the right dose at the right time every day.

What steps will I take when taking this medicine?

Many anxiety medications are also depressive. Likewise, screening for side effects, avoiding alcohol and using heavy equipment can be very important. Side effects can include dizziness and drowsiness.

Do I have to stop taking medicine?

Some anxiety medications can have poor interactions with other medicines, herbal medicines, and even providers. This is very valuable information for patients who need anxiety medication.

How long will I take this medicine?

Many types of anxiety medications are addictive. Therefore, doctors only prescribe it for short-term use. Patients must be aware of the risk of addiction and realize the need to avoid using it after some time.

What results should I see?

Anxiety medicines are not intended as a panacea. In most cases, they must reduce the worst symptoms and allow other forms of treatment.

What else will I do?

In most cases, anxiety treatment is said to be a complement to other forms of therapy that can help patients regain control of their lives. Other treatments for anxiety disorders can be very valuable.

Patients who are given knowledge and data about anti-depressant medicines are one step ahead in fighting their disease. If most people take the right steps to offer research and other treatments, they can overcome the symptoms that are controlled by their lives.

Children's data and anti-anxiety drugs It is unfortunate that children sometimes have anxiety disorders. However, children are often limited in their treatment choices, especially in terms of medication, unlike their adult counterparts. Children and anxiety treatment do not always go very well.

Although this drug can be very effective for most adults with anxiety disorders, some of the most common medications are not recommended for children with the same condition.

It must be determined carefully whether children and anxiety medications should be combined. Although treatment is sometimes necessary, doctors usually consider the risks of the benefits of determining whether anxiety medication and children should be shared.

If other treatments are promising, your doctor will likely recommend them rather than treatment. This is especially true for very young children.

It should also be remembered that children's medicine and anxiety have different meanings from adults. Children's bodies develop rapidly and can sometimes react differently to pharmaceutical products.

In most cases, the dose is very different from the dose for adults. When potential addictive substances are needed, doctors usually monitor children's use very closely. Some forms of treatment, such as psychotherapy are also often recommended to help young children manage and resolve anxiety disorders.

While most doctors prefer to treat children with anxiety disorders without medications, they are sometimes needed. In this case, several drugs are often used to treat children with anxiety disorders.

When combining child medicine and anxiety, selective serotonin reuptake inhibitors or SSRIs are the most commonly prescribed form of the drug.

The National Medicines Institute of National Mental Health includes several SSRIs that have also been shown to be beneficial in young children when children and anxiety medications need to be mixed. The most popular brands used by young people include:

- **Anafranil** - This is used in the treatment of Obsessive-compulsive disorder in children aged ten years and over.

- **Luvox** – This SSRI is used in children aged eight years and over.
- **Tofranil** - This drug is usually prescribed for bedwetting in children as young as six years.
- **Zoloft** - This SSRI is used to treat OCD in children aged six years and over.

If it turns out that children and restless drugs need to be mixed to make treatment more effective, parents will usually find that it doesn't need too long to use. Sometimes young people can benefit from relieving symptoms of this drug, which helps other forms of treatment.

Long-term effects of anxiety treatment Anxiety disorders are almost always treated with medication. However, people with generalized anxiety disorder, post-traumatic stress, or other groups will usually find that medication is not the only medicine.

Because anxiety medications can have many long-term disruptive effects, most patients and doctors prefer to use them only in acute situations or as a step to close the gap.

Why are drugs important?

Although it is important to look for the long-term effects of anxiety medications, these drugs are important. They are very often used in emergencies to relieve patients of their symptoms immediately. Medications such as Xanax and Valium can cause immediate acute anxiety. For example, given the acute crisis, you will feel relief in less than two hours in most cases.

Because these drugs eliminate symptoms and allow patients to focus on other coping mechanisms, they are considered to be very beneficial for a short time even in an emergency. They are sometimes needed for short-term daily use, especially when the effects of anxiety are large or cause daily routine problems for patients.

What are the consequences?

Because of the long-term effects of depression medications, they are usually only indicated for short-term use. These drugs are technically suppressive, which can cause addiction.

Most doctors prescribe medicines such as Librium and Ativan for temporary use to avoid the problem of addiction. Including addiction, some other long-term effects of anxiety medications can also focus on memory loss.

Anxiety medications can also have some unpleasant side effects in the short term. Because this medicine hurts, people can get tired, dizzy, and tired. Additional side effects include upset stomach, nausea, and sexual problems.

Avoid the long-term effects of anxiety drugs. These drugs are often used to help patients with anxiety disorders to relieve their symptoms in the short term. They are usually prescribed along with other therapies, including psychotherapy.

Patients are strongly advised to learn treatment techniques that do not require drug intervention to avoid the long-term effects of the drug. They are usually taught in counselling courses and can be given through meditation, relaxation, and other forms of self-help.

At least this can be a very difficult way to live with anxiety disorders. Although medicines are useful for treating certain symptoms, they are usually not the best way to treat it. To avoid the long-term effects of depression medications, it is often important to use other forms of therapy.

NATURAL THERAPY TO WORK WITH ANXIETY

Anxiety can be expressed as another physical symptom, which expresses general symptoms such as physical, mental, and psychological feelings that are further notified below:

1. Sensory nerves

2. Feeling without skills

3. There is an immediate threat, panic or destruction

4. Increased heart rate

5. Shortness of breath

6. Sweating

7. Shivering

8. Feeling tired or weak

9. Focus on the problem or think of something other than the current problem.

You will also find that there are many types of anxiety disorders, including social anxiety problems (social phobia, social hiding), panic disorder (extreme periods of intense anxiety, anxiety of pain (in case of anxiety, you might feel uncomfortable), and strong problems worry.

Recommended for doctors: You feel overly anxious and disruptive to work, interpersonal relationships, or other parts of your life. You are stressed, have problems with alcohol or drugs, or have other problems with mental well-being and anxiety. You think that your anxieties are related to your health problems. Immediately seek first aid with thoughts of suicide or suicidal behaviour.

And the stressful conditions of life - changes in family or work, families with death or birth, many people - can make symptoms worse. They suggest that psychotherapy (speech therapy) helps you find the roots of anxiety and learn how to work. Medications may be recommended in some cases, but there are many natural ways to eliminate anxiety.

Intestinal Relations: If you know how our digestive system is healthy and directly related to our mental health and whether you have celiac disease, food allergies, irritable bowel syndrome or other stomach disorders, you might also have a mental illness.

Effects on the digestive tract and immune function help in the development of intestinal microbes that make up the brain and neuroactive compounds from intestinal microbes, including both, which work simultaneously on brain neurotransmitter metabolites, intestine, not the brain.

Also, about 50% of neurochemicals, such as dopamine and most serotonin, originate in the intestine and regulate appetite, abundance and digestion. The role of microbes has recently been investigated by basic psychiatry because of the possibility that these chemicals could arise. These brain chemicals are produced in our intestinal bacteria and are related to the role of depression and anxiety.

Vitamin

Folic acid helps in the production of serotonin and complex carbohydrates produce serotonin. Serotonin is a chemical that produces neurotransmitters throughout the body as an emotional balance. Magnesium often has no anxiety, so make sure your diet contains some magnesium-rich foods.

Vegetables

Eat asparagus, oranges, pumpkins, and sweet potatoes with your folic acid and grains and starches like your complex carbohydrates. It also helps get enough vitamin C (eat fruit!) Zinc (cashew, friend). Learning how to eat rainbow vegetables can improve your emotions. Choose additional foods such as avocados, nuts, citrus fruits, complex carbohydrates, and healthy proteins to reduce anxiety, advises nutritionist Amy Bell. And if you want to learn that research shows that nutrition does not disappoint us, choosing your diet makes sense.

He drinks herbal tea

Chamomile tea can affect our body. Chamomile tea shows a significant reduction in anxiety symptoms within a few days, it seems to act on the body's main stress hormones and has the effect of controlling cortical alcohol.

Wow, traditional black-eyed Polynesians can also help relieve short-term and fresh stress, but it tastes good for tomorrow, but you can find it in supplements, tinctures, or tea (I like tea cards for stress relief), learn more about Herbs here the concept of green life.

Try it for a while if you drink regularly and see how you feel. Read why alcohol can reduce stress in some people, but not in others.

Food supplement

Many nutrients on the market can help reduce anxiety: use poppy seeds, delicate plants that taste like caramel, can be used with cocktails, fast food, or in combination with safe hot chocolate, which is popular. Our adrenal glands (development of all our stress hormones).

CHAPTER FIVE

RESPONDING TO ANXIETY

Everyone sees anxiety as a debilitating feeling that arises in inappropriate moments. People with chronic anxiety are far from getting rid of emotions that interfere with their lives. Whether it's asking someone for a ball, getting on a plane, preparing for an interview, or introducing yourself to a new crowd, most people are afraid in this scenario. While the effects of anxiety and symptoms vary from person to person, people with problems such as shaking hands, weak knees, sweaty palms, and heartbeat and high blood pressure experience a variety of terrible symptoms.

As a result, most people tend to avoid depression rather than deal with it. Although considered largely dangerous, many believe that anxiety can play a key role in improving one's work. Anxiety is a natural emotion that, when used properly, can lead people in the right direction and has a positive effect on worsening their condition. So it all depends on how the person concerned responds to the state of concern.

To avoid anxiety, reject opportunities and avoid decisions that bring them out of their comfort zones. They mostly see stressful events as threats (real or imaginary), not challenges.

Interestingly, in most cases, such an event does not indicate a lost cause. Anxiety is not always a bad thing; People who regard stress changes in life as challenges tend to increase their energy because of anxiety. In this way, awareness of the inputs and emotions of these emotions can enable a person to focus on the effects of alleviating sadness, and to present themselves better.

If someone has a dangerous or threatening biological situation, The fight or flight reflex begins in response to threats. This stress response is usually called anxiety. When anxiety mounts, you can feel trapped in a crisis. Fortunately, this condition is often not life-threatening.

The act of absorbing anxiety

There are two ways to respond when anxiety knocks on the door. While one involves escape, avoidance, and denial, the other involves absorbing the discomfort. If you realize that anxiety offers opportunities for efficiency, you can examine the positive aspects of anxiety.

It can also help relieve anxiety symptoms and are not beneficial in the long run. Although it may be difficult to do this in the first few attempts, you will gradually learn to turn anxiety and nervousness into jet propellers that allow you to aim high in the sky.

Anxiety, according to the American Psychological Association, is defined as feelings of tension, anxious thoughts, and physical changes such as high blood pressure.

If you can overcome anxiety, you or they are vulnerable to the negative effects of these emotions. If there is severe anxiety in every area of life, someone at full speed can develop anxiety disorders.

NATURAL SUPPLEMENTS FOR ANXIETY

Anxiety is a normal stress response and can be in some situations useful. For example, when you take a test or speak, your anxiety motivates you to prepare carefully. However, if your anxiety interferes with your daily routine and lasts more than six months, your doctor may need to help you determine whether you have an anxiety disorder or not.

Regardless of whether you have a complete anxiety disorder or only temporary anxiety, you might want to try to relieve your anxiety symptoms with certain supplements that occur naturally. There are some of the best natural treatments for depression on the market today. Some of these supplements work instantly, while others can help reduce depression over time.

Passion herb

The aerial part of the system is used to produce medicinal products. This herb is used against insomnia, gastrointestinal complaints, depression, GAD and drug elimination.

A list of solid natural remedies looking at the scientific evidence for passionate interest tends to be a concern. We also state that passionflower can sometimes relieve anxiety symptoms and certain prescription drugs.

Passion herb contributes to rest and natural sleep without feeling "sedated" and can help lower blood pressure. The calming properties of Passionflower allow the nervous system to relax and improve sleep.

In combination with other sedatives such as chamomile, hops, coffee, skull and valerian, passion flowers increase harmony and relaxation. Passionflower can be consumed in 250 mg or 1 ml tincture capsules, or 4 to 8 grams per day.

Because passionflower causes drowsiness, don't take sedatives while drinking. Remove the flowers of love at birth. Don't take passion interest for more than a month at a time.

In most cases, passionflower is safe if consumed for less than two months. This can be dangerous if consumed in large quantities. There are also side effects such as fatigue, dizziness, nausea in poor balance, vomiting, painful blood vessels, drowsiness and rapid pulse.

Coffee

Coffee has been used in the South Pacific Islands for more than 300 years. Much research has been done on the potential of coffee to reduce anxiety. There is strong evidence that coffee is superior to placebo and is by tricyclic antidepressants (Assendin and Norpramin) and weak benzodiazepines (Xanax) in the treatment of anxiety.

Coffee can be seen as a capsule, tincture, or extract form. There is no standard dose, and clinical trials have used doses ranging from 210 mg to 400 mg daily. Talk to your doctor before drinking coffee.

The Food and Drug Administration has warned of the possibility of serious liver damage from coffee. However, coffee sales are not prohibited in the United

States. I will not use coffee, especially if you have liver problems or if you take drugs that damage the liver. Some possible side effects include blurred vision, vomiting, loss of appetite, and breathing.

Valerian

Valerian is a wild plant that grows in moist places with pink or white flowers. Many studies have been found about the effects of valerian on sleep and an increase in valerian anxiety, moods, general well-being and insomnia.

People in Europe have been treating nervous anxiety, anxiety and nervous irritation for menopause for more than 100 years. Valerian was even used as a sedative to treat shooting forces during the First World War. Many people use valerian as a tincture or capsule. If you have insomnia, it should be taken 30 to 90 minutes before going to bed at night. For anxiety, two or three doses should be taken throughout the day.

Valerian is generally considered safe in the recommended guidelines. Start with a low dose and gradually increase the dose. Severe headaches, vomiting, nervousness, and palpitations can have side effects. However, controlled studies are quite vague about the side effects of valerian and report that they are small.

L-theanine (or green tea)

It helps you relax and calm your mind. L-theanine is involved in the production of GABA, a soothing neurotransmitter. GABA also helps neutralize glutamate, an exciting brain chemical.

Research has shown that L-theanine decreases heart rate and increases blood pressure, and many small studies have been found in people who reduce anxiety.

In one study, susceptible subjects were more relaxed and focused during the test if they had previously used 200 milligrams of L-theanine.

L-theanine is healthy for most people. Many people may experience irritation and constipation in the stomach.

Lemon balm

Lemon balm has been used since the Middle Ages to relieve stress and anxiety and support sleep. Lemon balm is a delicious, slightly warm herb that also functions as a mild antidepressant. In one study, those who used standardized urea extract (600 mg) were calmer and more informed than those who used the placebo.

Lemon balm is sold as a tincture, capsules, and tea, often combined with other soothing herbs such as hops, passion flowers, chamomile and valerian.

Grilling a lemon is generally safe, but there are side effects of increasing anxiety in people who roast too much lemon. Take smaller doses to continue. If you are pregnant, use only half of the recommended amount.

Chamomile

Chamomile has been used in various health conditions for thousands of years. Currently, it is used for insomnia, depression and digestive disorders. Some chamomile compounds bind to the same brain receptors as drugs like Valium.

In a study at the University of Pennsylvania Medical Center in Philadelphia, eight-week patients with GAD added a significant reduction in anxiety symptoms compared to patients treated with placebo. Chamomile can be taken as a liquid extract, capsule or tablet.

Side effects include allergic reactions such as rashes, swelling in the throat, shortness of breath and anaphylaxis. Such side effects can occur in people in the daisy family who are allergic to these plants.

Omega-3 fatty acids (fish oil)

Omega-3 is important for normal brain function. Both contain EPA and DHA and are important for stress management. There is the first indication that they affect the development of serotonin.

Scientific studies show that fish oil has a positive effect on the treatment of anxiety. A study found that students who consumed omega-3 fatty acids mixed in 2.5 milligrams per day for 12 weeks were less afraid than placebo students.

For most people, fish oil is healthy when consumed in low doses. There are several safety problems when consumed in high doses. Don't consume more than three grams a day.

Many side effects include stains, shortness of breath, boils, vomiting, loose stools, rashes and nosebleeds. Taking this supplement with food can reduce these side effects. Don't take fish oil supplements if you are allergic to seafood.

Vitamin B complex

B1 (thiamine) can help reduce depression and anxiety. Vitamin B6 (pyridoxine) supports the synthesis of natural antidepressants such as dopamine and norepinephrine. The body needs B6 to produce serotonin.

Vitamin B12 (cobalamin) causes relaxed irritability, increased concentration, increased strength and a balanced nervous system.

Vitamin B3 (niacin) maintains and calms nervous feelings.

Group B vitamins are burned and consumed in high amounts during high stress. Studies show that most mentally ill people lack one or more B-complex vitamins. Studies also show that B vitamins are natural stress relievers, and insufficient stress can cause anxiety.

The recommended use is to consume 100 mg of the vitamin B complex, which is excreted every day after eating. It is recommended that you take 100 mg of Niacinamide Vitamin B3 three times a day if you experience a very tense time.

Vitamin B-complex is safe for most people. However, some people may experience side effects of vitamin B12 such as diarrhoea, blood clots, itching, and severe allergic reactions.

Long-term use for more than a year can cause side effects of vitamin B6, causing serious nerve damage. If you stop taking supplements, the symptoms usually stop. Some effects include sores on the skin, resistance to heat, acid and vomiting.

I chose them as the best natural anxiety supplement because they have been studied more closely than other natural supplements. They also proved effective in controlling anxiety.

However, there are other natural supplements for depression, such as 5-HTP, Rhodiola, L-Arginine, L-Lysine and L-Tyrosine, GABA, St. John's Wort, SAMA, Vitamin E, Track Minerals.

They are often used for anxiety, but have not been well researched. They continue to undergo clinical trials because of its alarming effectiveness. So my list of the best natural food supplements for depression is up to work further: passion interest, coffee, valerian, L-theanine, urea, chamomile, omega-3 and vitamins from complexes that are affected by B.

Talk to your doctor first if you are thinking about herbal preparations for anxiety treatment, especially if you are taking other medications. The interaction of herbal supplements and certain drugs can cause serious side effects.

Talk to your doctor if your depression affects daily activities. More serious forms of anxiety usually require medical or psychological counselling to improve symptoms.

THE MOST POWERFUL VITAMIN FOR ANXIETY AND STRESS

The best panic attacks are normal and can be easily integrated into our lifestyle. You work with your body to control your anxiety symptoms, and we hope to eliminate them. However, unlike most anxiety medicines, these drugs get to the bottom of the problem and help you deal with your anxiety.

Vitamin anxiety works by controlling hormone levels and metabolism. This is a good and effective way to control anxiety and symptoms. They occur naturally in the food you eat, and you can add this vitamin to your body for maximum effect.

Let's look at these vitamins for anxiety: B vitamins for anxiety Group B vitamins play an important role in the functioning of the central nervous system because a deficiency of these vitamins often causes anxiety, depression, and stress.

Together as a B complex, B vitamins work best. You control your neurotransmitters, including serotonin and dopamine, and your moods and reactions when you face stress and anxiety.

Vitamin B-1 (thiamine) increases your strength and mood; Vitamin B-3 (niacin/niacinamide) reduces symptoms of panic and anxiety and helps you recover quickly after a panic attack. Vitamin B-6 (pyridoxine) has a variety of functions in the body, including the promotion of a healthy immune system, heart and circulatory system.

It also greatly affects the nervous system by controlling the body's dopamine and gamma-amino-butyric acid (GABA), which are responsible for periods of self-confidence, protection, and rest. Vitamin B-8 (inositol) has been highlighted as a good alternative for the treatment of anxiety, panic attacks, depression and some phobias in patients with fluvoxamine. It also affects the nervous system.

All you have to do now is love small, reliable vitamin C, right?

It is also known for treating common cold and scurvy and has an important relationship with stress relievers and anxiety. It can be extracted alone or from a multivitamin supplement. A hormone called cortisol is released by the body during anxiety or stressful events. This triggers your startup survival response.

Ideally, this should result in a rapid outbreak in such a situation with high alert. Then you have to release it through physical activity. This causes the degeneration of cells, bones, and muscles through cortisol. Drain the body's supply of vitamin C and damage the immune system.

Equipping your body with vitamin C can reverse this process, increase your body's metabolism, and thus reduce the negative effects of stress and anxiety.

Anxiety vitamins - B vitamins and vitamin C - are essential for effective bodily functions, because they regulate chemicals and neurotransmitters that generally keep your body healthy and consistently alleviate your anxiety symptoms.

So make sure that regardless of the panic attack that you plan to use for anxiety disorders. This, of course, works with your normal bodily functions to free you from anxiety.

CHAPTER SIX

COSTS OF NOT OBTAINING ANXIETY ATTACK TREATMENT?

You should not delay seeking help or consulting a doctor, because our company guarantees that only weak people try to help them. Removing anxiety attacks can cause lifelong misfortune. That's not worth it! Without treating anxiety, anxiety can increase and worsen. Your daily routine can be affected by attacks that don't exist.

This should turn to your head; there is no other way to be productive, healthy and happy. However, medical assistance in the form of anxiety attacks is needed if symptoms appear as soon as possible.

Sometimes anxiety can be caused by using a substance or condition, and anxiety therapy may not be needed, and all you have to do is stop using offensive substances.

Anxiety disorders such as drug use or natural remedies (e.g. acupuncture, herbal remedies, acupressure, exercise, aromatherapy, herbal remedies, dietary support, etc.) are not clinical.

Delayed anxiety therapy can cause agoraphobia and isolation. Panic attacks and agoraphobia are often closely related because these disorders have the same symptoms like shortness of breath, dying, madness, and heart attacks. When a person lives his life, it seems that he does not live his life alone, but only sees. This is also known as derealization. This feeling is intensified, and the person concerned will eventually withdraw from all forms of social interaction.

Delayed treatment can worsen your condition and cause more frequent and prolonged seizures than before. Anxiety disorders are related to depression, which can cause more depression. Depression is often the result of someone's fatigue from chronic anxiety which is usually associated with anxiety/panic attacks.

Experiencing depression and permanent anxiety can damage anyone who makes the victim unable, and thoughts of suicide are not uncommon.

Studies show that people with panic disorder are far more likely than people who don't try to kill themselves. Studies show that 20 per cent of panic attack patients risk suicide due to depression.

Increasing the production of adrenal hormones is one of the many changes that can occur due to stress. Lifts trigger the most painful effects of panic attacks. This also creates nutritional deficiencies. When a person suffers from long-term stress, nutritional deficits affect their health.

When suppressed by emotional or physical stimulation, many changes in the body disrupt the physical balance. Most researchers say that stress accounts for up to 80% of all serious illnesses.

Studies show that some believe that food shortages and related imbalances in body chemistry are caused by chronic anxiety attacks in thousands of Americans. Some people with excessive or unrealistic anxiety, chronic tension, cramps and sleep disorders may have serious magnesium and calcium deficiencies.

If a panic attack drug is not needed, this pressure can also eliminate the body's vitamins needed for normal functioning of the nervous system. Vitamin B-5 is known as an antistress vitamin. Both mental and physical health is affected by vitamin B-6.

Lack of vitamin B-12 can cause depression, indigestion, hallucinations, mood swings and nervousness. Folic acid causes depression and anxiety. Long-term stress weakens the body and makes it more susceptible to disease.

Excessive drug addiction to treat anxiety can be a problem because, although it is not synonymous with addiction, a person does not seek safer and more effective panic attack drugs that may be the main cause and can maintain or improve well-being.

The general appearance of people who are always anxious often changes to the appearance of being tired, anxious, and tired. Poor sleep for years, repeated negative thoughts, and constant anxieties can make someone look older than they are.

A person's life will be shortened by heart failure, ulcers, intestinal ailments, immune deficiency, and other stress-related illnesses as soon as they become a problem - unless treatment of anxiety attacks is started.

After all, it's best to seek professional support for an attack and then focus on yourself using natural remedies that can be used as long-term solutions to achieve full well-being.

BEARING WITH ANXIETY DAILY

Anxiety is not difficult to monitor. Did you know that more than 40 million people experience symptoms of anxiety in the United States alone? Those who are agitated often experience depression twice as likely to maintain anxiety and vice versa.

One of the best things you can do from the start is to understand different signs. The change between anxiety and panic attacks must also be recognized. The easiest way to do this is to recognize that anxiety symptoms are more common.

Tension headaches are one of the first things you should pay attention to. This is just one of the most common symptoms of anxiety. They are caused by some pressure that you meet regularly. You might want to look at all areas of your life if you already have a headache. One part can be a major cause of headaches.

Another common symptom of anxiety is a stomach pain. You might need to go to the bathroom again in the morning. Many people will decide that this is related to something they have consumed, but this bothers them with strong anxiety related to something in their lives.

Nausea and acid reflux can also occur. You can mess up everyday life and whatnot. Although easy to recognize, they are difficult to understand.

Boils are another thing to look for. Some of us develop ulcers because we often worry. The reason for this is that a number of these symptoms cause real health problems, which is why it is important to reduce your anxiety as soon as possible. This is easier said than done, but it can happen.

Restlessness and anxiety are other problems that are most easily recognized. Any frightened person is clear because he often shows, thinks about things and maybe even a little verbally.

Sometimes it's hard to get close to someone with these physical signs of anxiety. The truth is they can't help but be like that. If you can be with someone with anxiety, you might be aware of some of these problems.

Unfortunately, the longer you live with anxiety, the more visible symptoms of anxiety. You might think this is how everyone and you have something in common.

Although all of this is pretty scary, you should also see changes in the bathroom, restless nights, running thoughts, hyperventilation, tremors, muscle tension, low legs, and breathing. You can only see one or two of these anxiety symptoms, but you can also experience a lot.

People with anxiety also have recurrent panic attacks. Contrast with depression is that the signs almost always appear and never look better. The best place to start is to see what triggers the symptoms. See which ones disrupt your daily routine and are always positive. Even if this is the beginning, it can help you find your life again.

If you are nervous, happy to know that you can stop by remembering some physical signs of anxiety. Remember also that anxiety sometimes feels like you are nervous. It's also important to remember that generalized anxiety is a type of panic attack.

HOW TO SUPPORT PARTNERS WITH ANXIETY

I think we can all agree that supporting frightened friends is challenging. Those who panic can be irritated, frustrated, or scared. However, keeping your partner in anxiety is difficult for your partner. Couples are also confused, frustrated, and may feel out of control and helpless when their loved ones suffer. It is impossible to know how they can help or contribute to their healing and recovery in the future.

It's hard to live with someone with anxiety. Anxiety is frightening because the individual feels isolated and alone, and no one knows what he is doing. How can you do this when you are not afraid and worried?

Horrific decision making because it loses all confidence in itself and the ability to manage. Those who are affected believe that they always go out in the dark. We lack the confidence and courage to find a way out of normality. They just want peace and a calm mind.

Anxiety full thoughts continue to flood the mind, leaving little room for "just dreaming" without worrying about what happens when it happens, what if.

Even if you are distracted by watching movies or talking with friends, anxiety appears as a virus that has negative thoughts and scenarios all the time. Anxious patients may feel sorry for themselves, consider themselves a complete failure, or angry with others.

You can find the following help for people whose partners want to assess anxiety.

1. **Conscious Awareness:** When practised properly, conscious awareness opens the way to compassion and understanding. This happens when you recognize your

partner's worries and depressing thoughts. Knowing your reaction, tolerance, stamina, and vocabulary can help you reduce the potential for emotional tension when talking to a nervous partner.

2. As a partner of anxious people, you need to step back and understand that anxiety is not your problem. It is essential that you also monitor your thoughts and feelings and how your partner's anxiety can affect them. You must stop overreacting or become overly emotional when anxiety is triggered by your partner.

3. You must let the person talk about anxiety, but not exaggerating. Letyour's colleague spoke of concern. The disturbance is anxiety of feelings, so thinking about emotions is part of the healing process. However, thinking too much about your feelings when you start to get involved in your story can confuse and can increase anxiety.

It is important to emphasize the love and attention of your disturbed partner. You need to make sure they know that you are there for them and are ready to work together through their anxieties. You have to be gentle. Let your guide be empathetic and understanding.

4. Don't judge and try not to infer how your partner feels or thinks. Don't say "You have to think like this" or "You have to act like that". Your partner will have difficulty understanding their anxieties and their effects.

You don't need to find out why. Hearing things like "sucking" or "clicking" makes you more unwanted and unnecessary pressure and makes the situation much worse.

CHAPTER SEVEN

CHOOSING THE RIGHT PROGRAM - HOW TO CHOOSE THE BEST

There are thousands of services here, and all claim to be the best at calming anxiety. However, various stress solutions work better for different people.

How do you choose the best program for you? Ask yourself the following questions:

1. What are your anxieties?

Your anxiety behaviour must play an important role in your anxiety program. If you have situation anxiety, a program that only focuses on general anxiety may not be detailed enough. And if you experience panic attacks, phobia-based anxiety plans might not work. Pay special attention to your symptoms when choosing an anxiety plan.

2. Do you want a natural anxiety program or a prescription drug-based program?

Relaxation techniques, such as imaging and awareness are an integral part of many depression programs. Clear relaxation techniques help reduce stress habits easily and naturally.

Most activities focus on breathing. Soothing panic is only possible if you breathe properly. Most anxiety is exacerbated by shallow and rapid breathing. In just a few minutes, you can feel better by learning how to use deep breathing.

Fitness plays a major role in many programs. Finally, find chemicals that improve your mood and relax your brain. And the results of good practice continue throughout the day.

3. How easy is the process?

A good anxiety program offers step-by-step instructions and allows you to walk on your own. Think about it - if you are in a hurry with your diagnosis, you can feel more nervous! Look for anxiety plans that you know you must maintain.

4. Have you ever been anxious and depressed?

If so, you are not alone. Studies show that the majority of anxiety patients often show signs of clinical depression. If you are one of them, you may need to focus on caring for anxiety that solves all problems. Finally, depression has been proven to worsen anxiety and vice versa.

5. How long does this work last?

A good anxiety program will show you how to handle your anxiety behaviour and reduce it until you resolve the problem. Of course, you may need to learn what triggers and triggers your panic attacks from time to time, but you need to know how to reduce its effects immediately.

Even though it might not cure you, soothing depression can be done within minutes with the right method. You don't have to wait long to see the concrete results of your anxiety plan.

TEST-TAKING ANXIETY

All students feel very pressured to take the test. It is not uncommon for Student M to be stressed, and the more critical the exam, the greater the pressure. Most anxiety tests are natural and extraordinary. Common to all, except anxiety prevents you from conducting tests that are important to you.

Anxiety is a normal reaction to the stress experienced by everyone. The end anxiety test acts as a powerful motivator and makes learning more difficult as if you were not afraid.

On the other hand, overstress screening is not only painful, but it can also affect your ability to do your best. If depression affects your results on important tests like driving tests or entrance tests, your life can be a serious problem.

How do you know if you have a typical nerve beat or are afraid to take a more serious test? Think about the last important exam you took and ask yourself whether you experienced any of the following before or during the exam.

Mental health problems – Feelings of headache, vomiting or diarrhoea, sudden fever, excessive sweating, shortness of breath, mild or fainting, rapid heart breathing, muscle tension or dry mouth.

Emotional feeling - Feelings of intense anxiety, cheating, fainting, anxiety, restless laughter, crying, temptation to use something (drugs or alcohol) to calm you down or stop the exam.

Competitive thoughts - empty thoughts, focusing on confusion, negative self-talk, anxious emotions, negative associations with others, problems in organizing your thoughts.

If you have experienced many of these anxiety symptoms until they are severe enough to affect your ability to test, you may need help with an anxiety test.

What causes test anxiety, and why do some suffer while others remain calm?

Although there are many reasons to worry, the lack of a last-minute planner the night before or other bad behaviour in research and poor weather management are common reasons for worrying about a test.

Secondary sources of anxiety can be linked to other types of anxiety and stress. Will you experience a very difficult time in your life? Do you have other forms of anxiety? Panic attacks, sleep disorders, changes in appetite or problems with depression?

If you experience a lot of stress, this can cause more anxiety tests than usual. Many people are inherently more anxious and more often test depression and other anxiety symptoms.

Regardless of whether you are always very scared during your studies or during difficult times in your life, there are things you can do today to reduce your anxiety and improve your performance on important exams.

Here are some useful methods that you can use to monitor your test:

Be prepared

Be well educated and take the test with sufficient expertise so that you can remember important facts under pressure. Preparation will increase your confidence before the test and eliminate your anxiety.

Develop good study habits

You should avoid waiting until the last minute to study and not stay up late. If you have enough time, attend classes regularly, and do all your assignments, it will be much easier to prepare for your exam.

Practice relaxation

There are many simple sedative techniques that you can use to learn to calm yourself before and during a stress test. Try breathing exercises and methods for muscle relaxation, constructive thinking and imagination, exercise and a healthy diet. Simple changes like that will help you increase focus and reduce your anxiety.

If you feel nervous, rest and take a deep breath to calm down, don't be discouraged if your depression and nervousness cannot be completely cured. Focus on management. Remember that everyone is a little scared and that during training, you learn to deal with your anxiety and other stressful situations.

Here are some tips for practising your exam:

Create training settings that allow you to focus. Make sure it's calm, peaceful, dry, and comfortable. Remove interruptions and disturbances that are blocking focus. Don't research TV or radio, but you might want a soothing sound or fan to block unwanted noise.

Anxiety tests, like other anxiety disorders, can be managed effectively by making a few simple changes and using some useful strategies to manage anxiety when you start worrying.

PREPARATION FOR ANXIETY DIAGNOSIS

Anxiety disorders can occur in families at any age. Even children with the most active age groups are concerned. In general, anxiety is diagnosed when someone visits a doctor who specializes in treating anxiety and panic problems.

The doctor will ask patients questions about their lifestyle, history, climate, and daily activities due to anxiety disorders. For example, if there is a recent stressful event that is bothering them, the customer must explain this.

Some people find that changing their lifestyle, like moving to a new city, scares them. Changes in lifestyle, diet, and activity can cause anxiety. The doctor must examine the patient's care in an anxiety assessment to determine the underlying factors that cause anxiety and panic.

Diagnosing anxiety can sometimes reveal very hidden causes that we don't even remember. For example, a cruel child in childhood can find that because of his poor past, buried and hidden within himself, he reveals his ugly head and shows signs of anxiety.

Active depression treatment is carried out by doctors, not by our family doctor. Symptoms of anxiety can sometimes be so ambiguous that they can be ignored as a natural disease. If you believe you have anxiety and panic attacks, please contact your doctor. You must be responsible and always support yourself.

Patients are expected to be open to doctors during special anxiety assessments. If not, the topic of diagnosis is defeated. You are not only wasting money but also wasting time when you are not open and ready to learn about your anxiety diagnosis problem.

If you are embarrassed or don't want to accept that you need a diagnosis of a problem, you can still do a test to make sure you have real symptoms. You can learn more about anxiety attacks, understand yourself, and even prepare to take the next step to seek professional help through reading.

The first step is to get started. You don't need to rush to seek professional help if it frightens you. Try reading it, documenting your actions, wondering if you feel uncomfortable or react abnormally.

STOPPING ANXIETY ATTACK

Some people are often afraid, but some people are so worried that they begin to change their actions to deal with anxiety. Although this change might be better in some cases, e.g. If someone is afraid of their weight and starts to eat healthier and exercise, it can benefit them. This helps stop anxiety attacks. However, these changes are often negative because some people may not participate in activities that they normally like.

An attack or anxiety disorder can cause insomnia, excessive drinking, sex, eating and behaviour can be caused by one person. Anxiety can also make it difficult for people to maintain relationships. In severe cases, Anxiety can cause panic attacks, and it is difficult for people to avoid such attacks.

Some people may feel like having a heart attack or die while suffering from anxiety. It might be difficult to fall asleep at night, and this is considered to have a big adverse effect on your life. However, there are other ways to stop anxiety attacks. It is a good idea to seek help if these things keep you up at night, change your lifestyle, trigger panic attacks, or continue.

The first thing you can do is meet a therapist who can help you stop anxiety attacks. Cognitive behavioural therapy (CBT) is one of the main methods to combat anxiety attacks. Anxiety can mask underlying beliefs or deep sadness or trauma. CBT helps to understand what causes depression and has shown that many people seek effective treatment.

If therapy alone is not enough to stop anxiety, panic disorder or anxiety can occur. You should contact a doctor who can teach brain chemicals that contribute to anxiety attacks. When used together, CBT and drug work effectively to prevent anxiety attacks.

A little anxiety can be avoided by talking with friends, family, or school advisers. This way, you can understand how to deal with mild anxiety. If you cannot work and want to stay in bed, anxiety will not recede but will worsen your condition. Some of these strategies can help you avoid anxiety attacks or related feelings.

The first thing you can do is to avoid overeating and eat healthy foods to reduce your anxiety. Also, do not use illegal drugs or drinks because your condition will only worsen. The third thing you can do every day to stop anxiety attacks.

A 30-minute walk promotes the development of chemicals that make you feel good. You can also sleep more soundly at night. Meditation exercises such as yoga and tai chi can also help overcome anxiety. You can calm your mind with deep breathing and meditation.

You should see a therapist if your problem is not resolved by the method above. No matter how bad the anxiety is, there is always help. Medications are also a great way to get rid of depression and avoid panic.

CHAPTER EIGHT

THE BEST WAY TO TREAT THE SYMPTOMS OF ANXIETIES IN WOMEN

In everyday life, almost every woman in the world struggles with anxiety and stress. Unfortunately, sometimes it's difficult for people to deal with stressful situations. This can cause many psychological and physical difficulties. Although some people try to deal with depression due to alcohol and drug addiction, others depend on their treatment.

You don't need chemicals or medicines to get rid of anxiety symptoms in women. There are many ways to deal with stress and anxiety without addiction and treatment. You can use other anxiety management tips and holistic treatments from other anxiety symptoms in women.

A holistic approach is the best way to treat anxiety disorders effectively. Until we examine this approach, let's look at various symptoms of anxiety that occur in women. Common Anxiety Symptoms in Women Many people experience anxiety which includes some or all of the following anxiety symptoms. However, triggers play an important role in distinguishing panic or health anxiety from chronic anxiety.

For example, it is common to wake up from sleep when you feel like hearing strange noises in the middle of the night and pay attention to your muscular attacks and heartbeat. But when you sit in a cafe, it is very unhealthy and dangerous.

It is important to recognize the various situations and people that cause problems. You need to make sure you stay away from these situations and people. Specific ways to avoid stress in your life are also important. You need to recover from certain tasks, situations and routines if you do not want to take medication for your anxiety disorder.

You must focus on reorganization. This helps you to solve problems or problems with new approaches and perspectives. It is essential to examine how you react to certain situations when trying to treat anxiety symptoms in women. Priorities for different tasks must be prioritized individually.

You can even join a support group to deal with various anxiety symptoms that affect your life. With a support group, you share your concerns with like-minded people who have the same problem. If you want to treat anxiety symptoms without medication, you can focus on many different things to relieve stress.

There are some great stress management techniques such as relaxation, exercise, listening to music, laughing, watching your favourite movie, taking a walk in the park or at sea, and more. These simple techniques will best overcome the effects of your anxiety.

There are other ways to deal with stress and depression without drugs. This includes regular exercise, adequate sleep, good body nutrition and much more. The mind and body must be safe to deal with difficult situations correctly. Therefore, you need to consume lean protein, vegetables, whole grains and fruits to achieve long-term firmness.

You also need to exercise regularly so that your body's oxygen is maintained and let your brain work faster. The ideal way to deal with depression is to evaluate positively together. You should not worry too much. It is important to have a positive outlook on life.

However, you need professional help if you have chronic anxiety and stress and cannot eliminate the symptoms of generalized anxiety in women. You need to consult with a psychologist or psychiatrist to solve your problem.

DEALING WITH TEENS SUFFERING FROM ANXIETY DISORDERS

Anxiety is a normal response to stressful or dangerous situations. If someone is afraid of failing an exam, he will study harder, or if he is nervous about speaking, he will focus on preparing well for the speech.

In general, anxiety helps us stay focused and alert, but becomes frustrated when ANXIETY becomes excessive or irrational, which prevents you from working normally in everyday life.

People with anxiety problems or disorders suffer from symptoms such as tremors, sweating, throbbing, vomiting, numbness, shortness of breath, dizziness, unpredictable obsessive-compulsive thoughts, loss of focus and feeling crazy during an anxiety attack. Symptoms of anxiety or depression often start in early childhood or adolescence.

The young years are considered the most important years in human development. When the problem of anxiety takes their victims and destroys this important phase, a person's life can be miserable. If they are not heard and cared for, their interactions and school work may be disrupted.

Teens with anxiety become nervous, even if they do not have anxiety attacks. A simple anxiety of another depressive episode will make your life miserable. You can learn not to go to school or avoid everyday situations that can cause other anxiety attacks.

Models to avoid and anxiety future attacks can cause depression and other problems if left untreated. Proper anxiety management is important if you want to help teens with anxiety problems solve their anxiety problems.

Only a small proportion of adolescents receive psychiatric treatment, perhaps because the correct diagnosis was not made and the condition is ignored.

Anxiety disorders in adolescents can be difficult to diagnose, but when properly diagnosed, teens with anxiety problems usually respond well to treatment.

One of the best mental disorders that can be treated is an anxiety disorder. Teenagers with anxiety symptoms must be diagnosed by students who are qualified to deal with anxiety problems. Treatment for anxiety disorders continues to increase, and research is ongoing, and those who seek treatment will benefit from this therapy.

Support young people in dealing with stress. Stress is a major cause of anxiety, and teens and adults can also experience stress every day. You need to know how difficult it is to be a teenager and how stressful it is to do well in school, hang out with everyone, or fit in with your environment.

They may feel confused and unable to cope with the stress they experience at a young age and need help from people around them. Sometimes the problem is that not all teenagers with anxiety disorders are very open when they ask for help when stress is overcome, but they try to cover it up and suffer alone.

If young people can't control their stress, it can cause anxiety. Parents must be vigilant and know what is happening to their child. Parents should be able to find out if their teenagers are too stressed. It is best to monitor how stress affects your baby's emotions, behaviour, eating habits and overall health.

Listen to your child and pay close attention to signs of anxiety. Help your children and tell them that you are always there for them. Encouraging them to talk about things that stress them out is a good place to start helping teens with anxiety disorders.

Anxiety is a treatable disease, and young people with anxiety disorders must not suffer for the rest of their lives. Help your teenager regain his life and get rid of the devastating symptoms of anxiety.

MANAGEMENT OF ANXIETY WITH OTHER EMOTIONAL DISTURBANCES

There are various mindset in treating depression, as in other emotional disorders. Various consultants recommend behavioural changes such as relaxation therapy, ending thinking, modelling and behaviour training.

These techniques may be partially useful, but the lack of behaviour changes is that perceptions and mental conditions that cause anxiety may not be the focus of attention in treatment. Care must be mental rather than behavioural. In general, emotions are secondary and at the same time.

Some tips for anxiety management have been given above. Additional details and feedback are now available. Depression depends on the state of mind, as has been indicated. Therefore, treating anxiety must begin with confronting and assessing psychological anxiety. For example, this approach requires consideration of perception and interpretation of mental states.

Furthermore, conflict requires confident thinking. This serves to consciously direct your emotions inward and analyze them as objectively as possible. It tries to classify the basic ideas of perceived anxiety. For example, a young minister with high aspirations can become very anxious before his sermon.

This anxiety can be more than "stage terror". Even though he remembers unconsciously (as often happens), his mind can become a terror. He might have anxiety of the unimpressive; rejection of anxiety; anxiety of not being able to. A confrontation is a psychological act of honesty and courage.

The analysis is a more complex process than confrontation. This requires a critical examination of the mind to understand its source, reason and truth. For example, if you are afraid, you might feel guilty.

He will wonder why he is guilty or why he is guilty. On Sundays, he may not shake hands with church members or ask very simple questions to the economy class. He will ask if it's a good idea to feel this regret after making a mistake. In the first scenario, he might not have a real chance to shake his hand, so he doesn't feel guilty. However, he is not required to shake hands with men every Sunday.

Shaking hands is an act of mutual unity, not just religious activities. In the second case, he might have asked questions for which he did not know the answer to clarify the question or increase understanding so that he was not disturbed by other people's judgment.

It seems to be learning and growth. The person might not need to feel guilty in the two cases mentioned. Then he must ask himself how he can best understand the situation (i.e. in a rational and logical way). In both cases, mistakes are unfounded and must, therefore, be rejected. His thinking is flawed. His state of mind is morally groundless.

Therefore, this analysis involves a careful and thorough study of the dynamics behind mental conditions to assess the nature of these conditions. The roots of such diseases can be rooted in some childhood experiences. At this point, complex assessments and medical care may be needed.

Research encourages people to take psychological (objective) positions to resolve existing psychological states. When you question your emotions and understand the logic of experiencing anxiety, you often identify the source of your mental condition (when anxiety is situational).

Therefore, it is good for someone to discuss their concerns with close friends or professional partners in phase two of this conflict and assessment. Right, open interaction is very helpful.

This method of "confrontation and reflection" must be seen as a special type of cognitive process, namely self-examination. This treatment helps patients develop object-to-object relationships with anxiety (with its causal factors).

The victim can fight and fight, instead of distinguishing a person from anxiety, so that it can be said, "captured" by him. This psycho placement itself spreads some intensity of anxiety, but most importantly, it triggers the process of dispersion.

Patients must be "guardians" or "observers". Humans can now be separated psychologically from experience by creating a pseudo-objective position to determine the nature and source of disaster and to justify the conditions that cause such anxiety.

Such "objectification" - from subjective relationships with anxiety (and its prevalence) to fairly objective relationships - is essential for effective treatment of anxiety. Ignorance is only perpetuated and can even make the situation worse.

The essence of mental health is self-understanding. Self-optimization can only be stable based on self-image. Emotions are secondary; Cognitive is the centre. Emotions only reflect or express ideas and perceptions.

Emotions are not separate and distinct beings. They mainly depend on how and what you think. Therefore care must be largely mental. Emotional symptoms must be overcome indirectly by directly overcoming the mental state.

To change your mind, especially about anxiety, you need to maintain an appropriate mindset. Two approaches illustrate this approach. The next step is to estimate the problem. Many anxieties arises from the assumption of a future perspective, which leads to uncertainty and doubt.

You must focus on problems and challenges every day and try not to think and think too much about the coming days (this does not eliminate the need for proper planning). You must be prepared to train your mind to be proactive.

Second, a more general perspective needs to be developed. They research and evaluate problems and events in a wider area of "global villages" and "collective consciousness". Close and unjustified attention to personal information is usually a concern. Excessive focus on the details of life without respecting them in a broader context causes misunderstanding about what constitutes real value and real meaning.

In addition to previous observations about anxiety management, various practical steps can be taken to maintain anxiety control.

First, an alarming situation needs to be changed. For example, if you are ready to work on time, the hours must be set 30 minutes early.

Second, a daily to-do list must be made, preferably with the more demanding and demanding tasks listed above. Just mention what he could do that day.

Third, regular breaks and rest periods must be planned for each day. Walking outdoors can be soothing.

Fourth, adequate sleep is needed every night. A healthy body maintains a healthy mind.

Fifth, a regular exercise routine must be used. Exercise is very important. Exercise increases stability and endurance.

Sixth, you need to learn to talk with close friends about your problems and problems. Direct and open interactions, in turn, can be very therapeutic.

Seventh, holidays must be taken regularly, and everyday life changes.

Eighth, medical examinations must be scheduled regularly. Anxiety can be based on physiology or chemicals.

Ninth, we must adopt the tradition of listening to melodic music. The right type of music is soothing and calming.

Tenth, you need to form a circle of good friends. Socialization training has emotional strength and stimulation. Someone gets a sense of belonging. A good mental health support system is also important.

Eleventh, there must be a hobby. Interest and excitement produce positive and directed energy.

Twelfth, nutritious and healthy food can help relieve anxiety. In addition to organic foods, nutrients such as vitamins B and D, omega-3 fatty acids and minerals such as calcium and magnesium must be included. Herbal teas like chamomile can also help.

CHAPTER NINE

TIPS TO REDUCE YOUR ANXIETY

For several days, most people face the consequences of anxiety. In some cases, excessive stress and anxiety can cause extreme anxiety. However, anxiety can cause changes and mental, physical, and behavioural problems. No matter what is important to you, you are not alone and can change it and feel better.

Various symptoms can occur when dealing with anxiety, e.g. These include mental and physical fatigue, regular headaches, excessive pressure or chest pain, back, vomiting, dizziness, inability to relax fully, and problems sleeping or sleeping.

These are the most common signs. You can only test one or more at a time. If you have high anxiety or generalized anxiety disorder, you might not even begin to make a list of the symptoms listed. The emotional pain you feel from your hand and wondering what happened to you can be devastating.

The good news is that improvements can be made that reduce your anxiety, relieve your symptoms, and help you live your life again, whether your anxieties are the result of phobias, illness, intimacy problems, or ongoing financial problems.

One of the biggest elements in reducing anxiety is focusing on your thoughts. I believe that a healthy body needs a healthy mind, and a healthy mind enables a healthy body to recover. This means that you need to take a closer look at your thought patterns and practice them deeper and more regularly. When you are worried, your mind is constantly overwhelmed. This is when the signs and feelings of anxiety begin to dominate your mind and body.

Here are the steps you can take to reduce your anxiety and take action:

Relax your mind:

This is an important step. We also think we are relaxed when sitting on TV or having a rumour when we talk to a friend. No matter how pleasant it is, that does not mean that these things allow the mind to relax. To achieve complete relaxation, you must spend at least 10 to 20 minutes every day.

During this time, it is best to be alone and use certain techniques that will help you relax more easily. You can try relaxation, deep breathing, visualization, yoga or meditation.

Choose the one that best suits you so you can easily maintain it. The basic idea is to have time for yourself without being interrupted so that you can relax and blow away all the tension from your body with your mind, body and soul.

Need time:

When you are worried, your mind often does not stop without perseverance. If you find it difficult when your anxieties or negative thoughts begin to calm down, let them pay attention to these thoughts or worries, make them physically, replace them with a picture of yourself and look happy and healthy.

Often you have to do this, believe that these thoughts will diminish with time. If you want, you can say it out loud: "I have now decided to relax", leaving aside negative thoughts that interfere.

Believe in yourself:

Sounds simple, but many people struggle with it. Know that you have the tools you need to feel yourself and be better. Believe in yourself and state yourself strong and capable. This is true if you don't believe in yourself and want to change your mind.

Remember your skills every day. Orally say to yourself: "I am strong and able to master any challenge." The more you say it and remember your skills, the more strength and skill you will feel when you need it most.

Look at your anxiety head:

It will be very helpful if you focus on your anxieties and check where they came from and what was possible for you in the beginning. I know you can argue that anxiety has no purpose other than making life difficult and painful, but anxiety is your body's natural physical activity and response to perceived threats.

If you are constantly nervous, this can help you look back on your original situation or other situations where you remember feeling anxious. If you are worried or anxious, anxiety can be created to protect and secure you.

For example, health problems can cause anxiety that you won't get sick. This can then be experienced by avoiding situations or events that put you in contact with germs, or by avoiding certain foods.

Lifestyle rating:

What we eat, drink and exercise directly affect the anxiety and symptoms that can be associated with it. Your body, mind, and cells need to be properly fed and oxygenated to feel and feel good. High sugar or caffeine intake increases anxiety and avoids symptoms.

After overcoming my anxiety, I noticed that my anxiety would increase immediately after drinking chocolate. This does not mean that you are high in caffeine, but it is an example of how eating or drinking can affect you. Pay attention to your daily diet and how you feel when you drink and eat these things.

You might find a connection between your depression and what you consume, or you might find something that can help improve your health and might disappear from your diet. Exercise also leads to coping with stress and mood swings.

Eating healthy, drinking more water, and being active for at least 30 minutes a day can help relieve pressure, improve body and mind, and just feel better.

Whatever action you choose, the goal must be consistent. Don't give up or don't give up unless you see immediate results. The symptoms associated with anxiety require time to develop, and it takes time to cope and alleviate them.

Take time every day to choose techniques that allow you to relax easily and often and understand what triggers your anxiety. Listen to your body, and it will always give you signals and signals to tell you what is wrong and what you can do to feel better.

You can face the challenges you face when you are consistent and you believe in yourself. Believe in yourself and your inner wisdom.

USE THESE IDEAS TO CONTROL YOUR ANXIETY

Physical anxiety cannot be avoided in the context of daily activities. However, if you feel anxiety controlling your life, you need to learn how to control it. This chapter helps you manage stress more effectively.

The first step in overcoming anxiety is to eliminate the causes that cause your nervous feelings. Think about and give a name to what your depression began. If you enter a name, you might notice it. So try to understand it and talk about it later.

Try yoga with a group of friends to get rid of anxiety. Yoga is ideal for freeing the mind from anxiety and focusing power on current tasks. This exercise will help you calm down mentally. You can even feel happy and comfortable.

Keep your daily stress away from depression. If your stress level is too high, your anxiety level will also increase. Try to delegate certain tasks to others and get rid of some of your responsibilities. Try to relax and have fun every day.

Take 20 seconds to freeze your hands and put them in your eyes to relax. Most patients with depression use this strategy to relieve stress quickly. Try this quick technique the next time you feel stressed.

If you can't control your anxiety, contact a professional. Sometimes we underestimate the things in our lives or don't take the time to take care of ourselves. Professionals can help you understand why and how much you care.

There are hot and cold drinks that can cause calm anxiety. Chamomile tea is an amazing stress reliever and can help overcome problems. Consider drinking chamomile tea today and see if this reduces your anxiety.

People with heart problems don't have problems talking to health professionals about it. Likewise, people with anxiety problems should have no problem talking to psychologists. This is just another type of medical problem, which is why an expert needs help.

To ensure that anxiety is successfully resolved, you must get enough sleep. Lack of sleep can also worsen depression and cause physical (pain) and psychological problems (loss of severity). Adults must sleep every day for 7 to 8 hours to overcome anxiety.

Find out what negative people you can do anytime. Negative people harm you. Surround yourself with friends who are optimistic about having a positive outlook on life. Try to convey one of your greatest anxieties to trusted friends and add as much as you can when you tell them. The more you repeat the story, the more stupid it seems, which helps you not to be too afraid.

One of the best ways to overcome anxiety is to learn what causes it. For example, you might feel stressed at work. Maybe you can work with your manager to find out how to find a new project if you have one. If you know the source of your anxiety, it can be removed.

It's easy to get rid of your anxieties from your chest by sharing them with others - whether it's people who are related to health, family members, or friends. It will be much more challenging to overcome your anxiety alone. Talking about these things can make you feel better and not be too nervous.

Keep yourself busy. Even if you lie down all day, think more about your depression. This can be very helpful to keep you busy and useful. Try simple tasks like cleaning the house or cleaning the garden.

If you are someone like millions of others who have chronic anxiety, you can find conversations with friends and family. You can express yourself to all your friends and family to counter the negative energy that comes from your anxieties.

Think positive about depression! Anxiety is often associated with negative thoughts and emotions. For starters, a smile can be enough to solve your problem. Focus on happy ideas and thoughts and avoid stressful situations or take them away if you can.

As mentioned above, anxiety in its softer forms is part of our daily routine and is only one of our things. If your anxiety prevents you from returning to normal, you need support or have to find a more productive technique. The tips and suggestions above will help you in this direction.

CHAPTER TEN

TIPS FOR ANXIETY SUFFERERS

Most of the world population currently have anxiety disorders. Family problems, financial problems, problems at work and various other factors cause anxiety. Anxiety is more common than previously thought. Usually, more than 10% of the world's population can be scared. Some common symptoms include palpitations, irregular breathing, and more.

Anxiety can be quite challenging to treat, and persistent treatment is needed to treat the symptoms. In addition to normal pharmaceutical treatments and treatments, some natural treatments are also beneficial for patients with anxiety. They can take the form of herbal products, social/comfort adjustments, or some physical regimes.

There are several natural ways (besides drugs) to get rid of tense nerves and control anxiety. Some herbal products are known to relieve anxiety-related symptoms with longer-lasting effects such as kava, valerian root, and arousal. Such herbs are considered successful and are part of many herbal stress treatment programs throughout the world.

Irregular symptoms such as shortness of breath, blunt head and neck, etc. Can be observed in patients with severe anxiety. Many self-control measures can help relieve symptoms and restore calm. Some measures of self-control effects include Breathing.

If an anxiety attack occurs, the ability to breathe normally is somewhat disturbed. At such times, you need to try to regulate your breathing. Then imagine something fun or something that makes you happy, blow like a birthday candle to control your breathing. This will work wonders for a while to control your anxiety attacks.

Talk to people you love or take a walk

Talking to someone near you can have a magical effect that significantly reduces the effects of anxiety attacks. Using this therapy to reduce and control anxiety is important for sharing your mental state and causing anxiety.

A short walk will help relieve anxiety. Brisk walking or even light jogging increases blood pressure, makes breathing difficult and increases blood flow to the brain. All these physiological changes help you control the onset of anxiety.

Vitamin

Vitamins have a positive effect on the treatment of anxiety. Adding vitamins b12 and b1 as a food supplement can help reduce anxiety.

Magazine

Anxiety can seriously affect people with minimal social contacts, such as prisoners and retired soldiers. Longer periods of depression cause anxiety. For patients with anxiety, it is advisable to write everything about yourself, such as feelings, thoughts, and even dreams, to write a diary.

These are some natural (non-drug) ways to reduce anxiety. It is recognized that they are usually not recognized by treatment and should not be considered as alternative treatments for anxiety. They can have additional values when used as add-ons.

FREQUENTLY ASKED QUESTIONS ABOUT HOW TO DEAL WITH ANXIETY

Previous chapters have shown a list of treatment options that will help you deal with anxiety naturally. To continue, here are some common questions (Frequently Asked Questions) that we believe can help you overcome your anxiety.

What is the difference between panic and anxiety?

Anxiety disorders are psychiatric problems associated with a person's negative thoughts. Panic, OCD, phobia, or post-traumatic stress disorder (PTSD) can cause anxiety.

Panic disorder is an anxiety disorder. It contains unexpected and extreme panic attacks that occur without reason. Someone who experiences a sudden panic attack, anxiety, or has severe chest pain, an irregular heart attack, nausea, or dizziness in addition to feeling torn, unreal, or crazy.

Can anxiety kill me?

No, anxiety cannot kill you because your feelings or episodes are not physically threatening, and your thoughts make it look deadly or threatening.

Can anxiety be hereditary?

The answer is NO, but a person may tend to develop anxiety disorders due to genetic factors. If you are closely related to someone with anxiety disorders, you are likely to be prone to anxiety.

What causes anxiety disorders?

Relatively, there are rare grounds for developing anxiety disorders. Such conditions are usually caused by a combination of stress, injury, hereditary disposition or lifestyle. This condition does not manifest overnight and may need some time to be properly identified because the symptoms are usually small and long before the condition develops.

Can I overcome my anxiety attack and become normal again?

Yes, you can overcome your anxieties. You will be able to overcome your anxiety if you know you have an illness and seek treatment. You need to learn how to deal with depression and prevent serious problems in the future.

Is it possible for a person to have more than one anxiety disorder?

Yes, a person can have two or more anxiety disorders. This is called comorbidity. They are usually grouped into groups. For example, agoraphobia can occur in many people with panic disorders.

Is agoraphobia a serious problem?

Severe anxiety refers to anxiety disorders that affect one's lifestyle. Because certain circumstances or situations are avoided through agoraphobia, the quality of life and daily life can be disrupted.

Is my stress disorder related?

Stress can be a factor or cause of your anxiety, although it may not be the only factor. However, this, of course, can weaken your determination to fight anxiety.

Am I the only one with this problem?

You are one of the millions of people worldwide with anxiety disorders. According to current data, one in four is estimated to suffer from anxiety.

CONCLUSION

Anxiety arises in various ways depending on the severity of the condition. This can start from worrying about something that happened to us, or something that we hope will happen to ourselves, but in the end, the anxiety disappears, or we learn to deal with ourselves.

The symptoms of anxiety can manifest themselves physically and psychologically. Anxiety disorders occur when our brain warns us of the perceived danger. In this situation, your body is ready to fight or fly. The brain, lungs and other body parts need to work faster and produce stress hormones and adrenaline to overcome them.

Based on risk perception, physical symptoms include diarrhoea, dry mouth, stomach discomfort, rapid heartbeat, palpitations, tightness and chest pain, shortness of breath and dizziness. Such physical effects can make anxiety disorders frightening and improve symptoms.

Psychological symptoms of anxiety include insomnia, irritability, anger, being unable to concentrate on various daily tasks, anxiety of insanity, anxiety of losing your mind and mental performance, and feelings apart from the fact that is impossible to control your actions.

In addition to anxiety symptoms, people may experience psychological symptoms such as constant anxiety that has nothing to do with your current situation. Others can be anxious because they are involved in stressful situations such as work pressure or connections.

Then anxiety symptoms can appear because you are worried about real or imaginary illnesses. Then your body always reacts to the perceived dangerous threat.

All of this psychological pressure can and will dramatically intensify anxiety symptoms.

These symptoms can be considered anxiety symptoms if they last longer or are severe, or if anxiety symptoms occur if they are harmless or stressed. If these anxiety symptoms interfere with your daily routine and activities such as work and social events, you are sure of the anxiety disorder.

Anxiety is a normal reaction to danger, as the world knows. Everyone is concerned about something at a particular point in their lives. However, depression often turns into something known as an anxiety disorder.

Even though you might have symptoms of anxiety, it is always a good idea to consult a qualified doctor who will then put you on the right path for healing to confirm your self-diagnosis. Your doctor must be able to diagnose your complaint if you are afraid. Most forms of depression therapy can be tried. It is a good idea to talk with a doctor, a psychologist who specializes in anxiety and panic disorder, before starting such a course. Because treatments can vary, tell your doctor that you suspect you have an anxiety disorder to identify your specific condition. After your anxiety is diagnosed, treatment can begin.

You might want to ask your doctor what anxiety medications to take, the side effects, and how they affect your lifestyle. Don't rule out alternative solutions - drugs may not have been fully proven to treat anxiety, but many people say this alternative treatment can help relieve anxiety symptoms.

14121998

Please kindly leave a sincere comment and don't forget to check my other books. Thank You.

www.ingramcontent.com/pod-product-compliance
Lightning Source LLC
Chambersburg PA
CBHW070657250726
48662CB00001B/170